THIS BOOK BELONGS TO

,,,

,,,

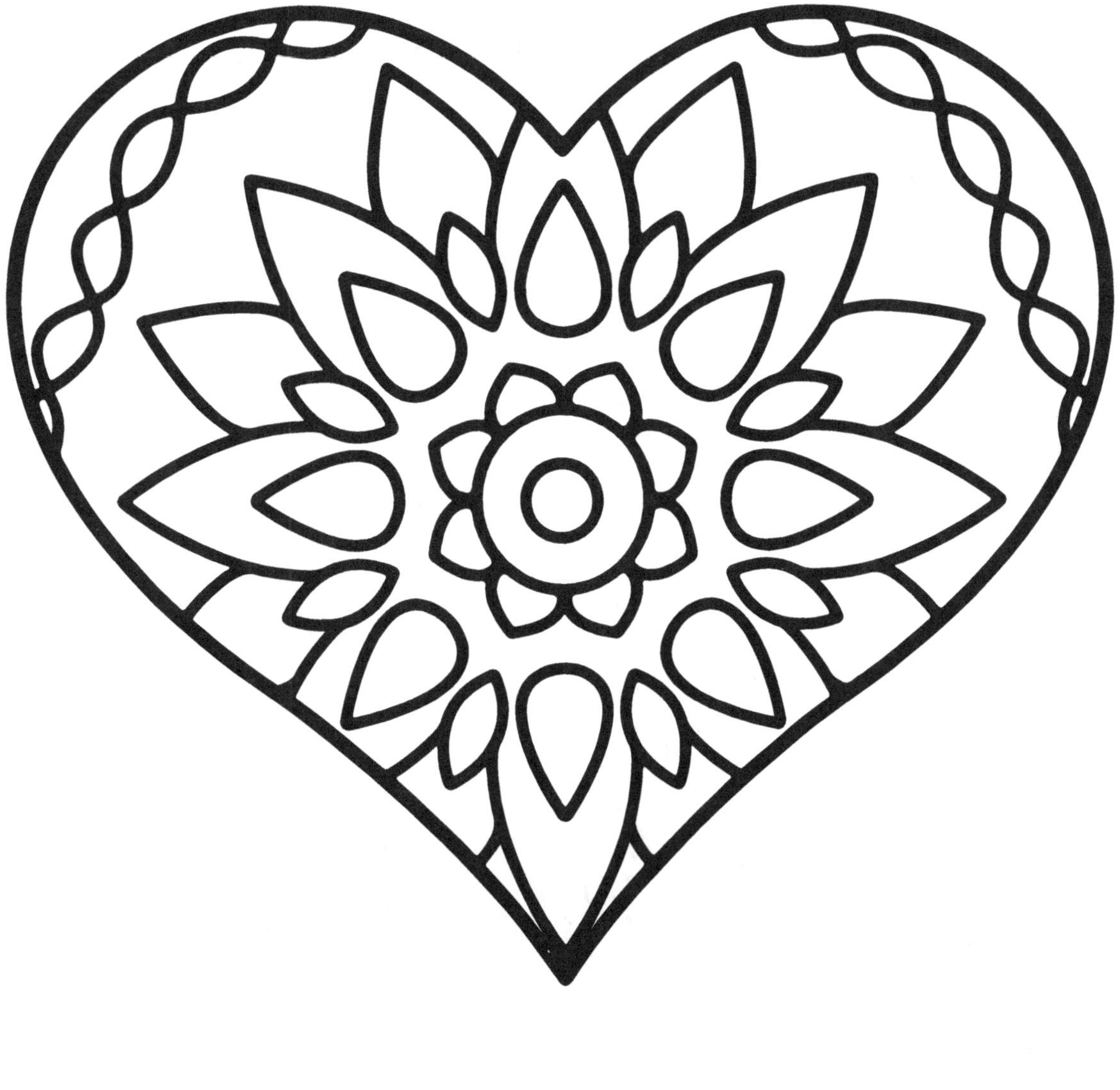

MANDALA HEARTS

by Little Mary

MANDALA HEARTS

by Little Mary

MANDALA HEARTS

by Little Mary

MANDALA HEARTS

by Little Mary

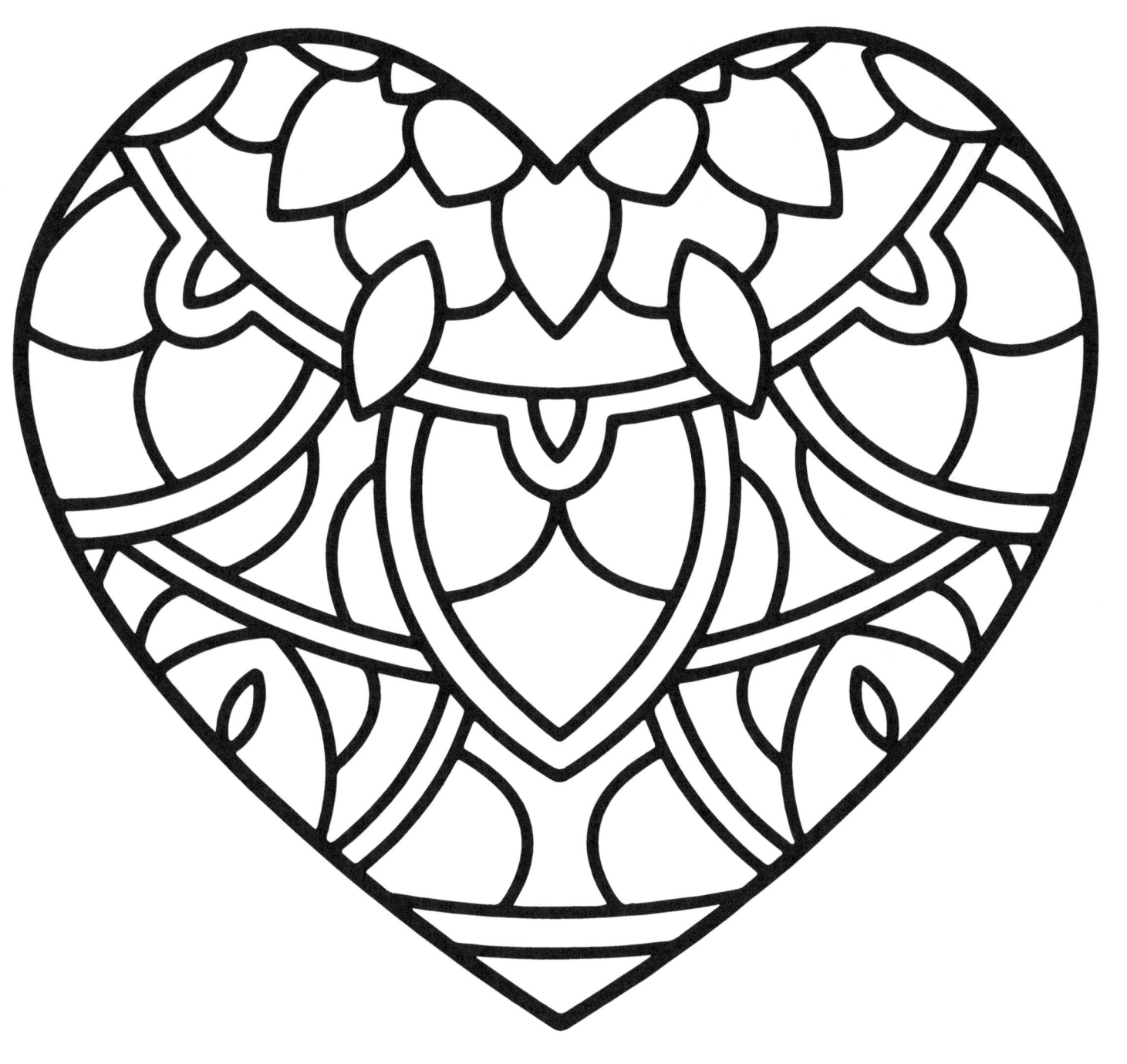

Mandala Hearts

by Little Mary

Mandala Hearts

by Little Mary

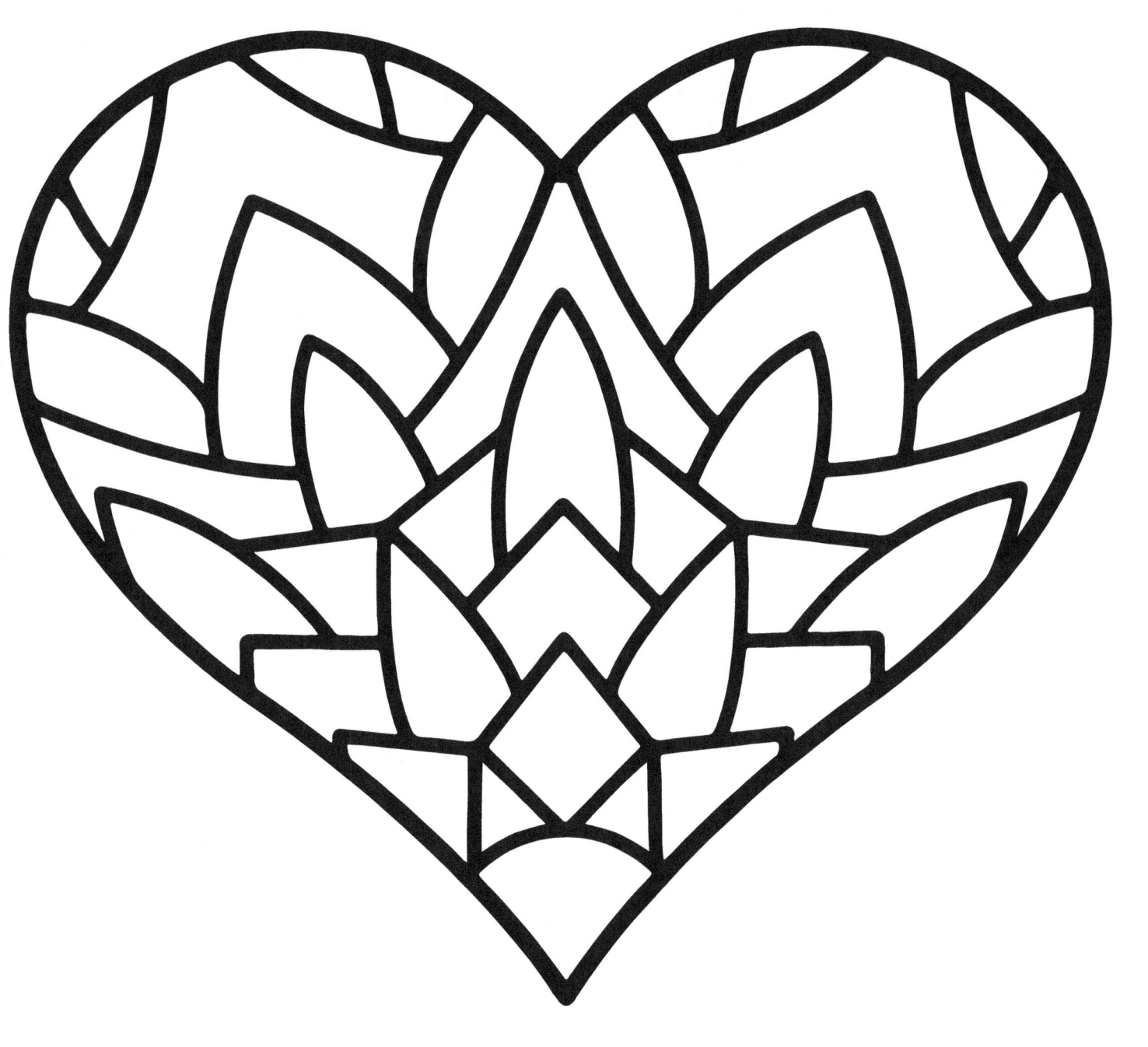

MANDALA HEARTS

by Little Mary

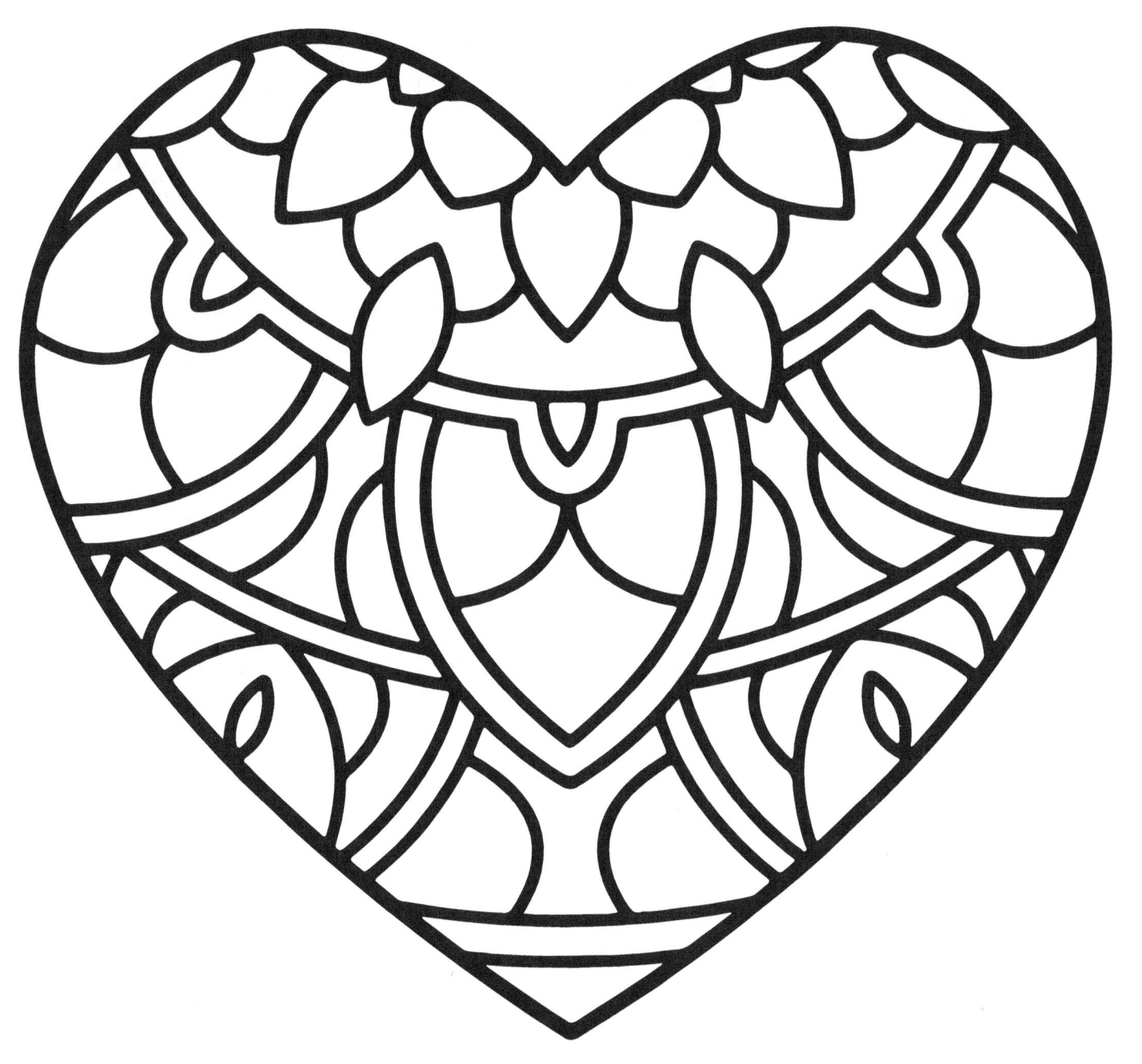

MANDALA HEARTS

by Little Mary

MANDALA HEARTS

by Little Mary

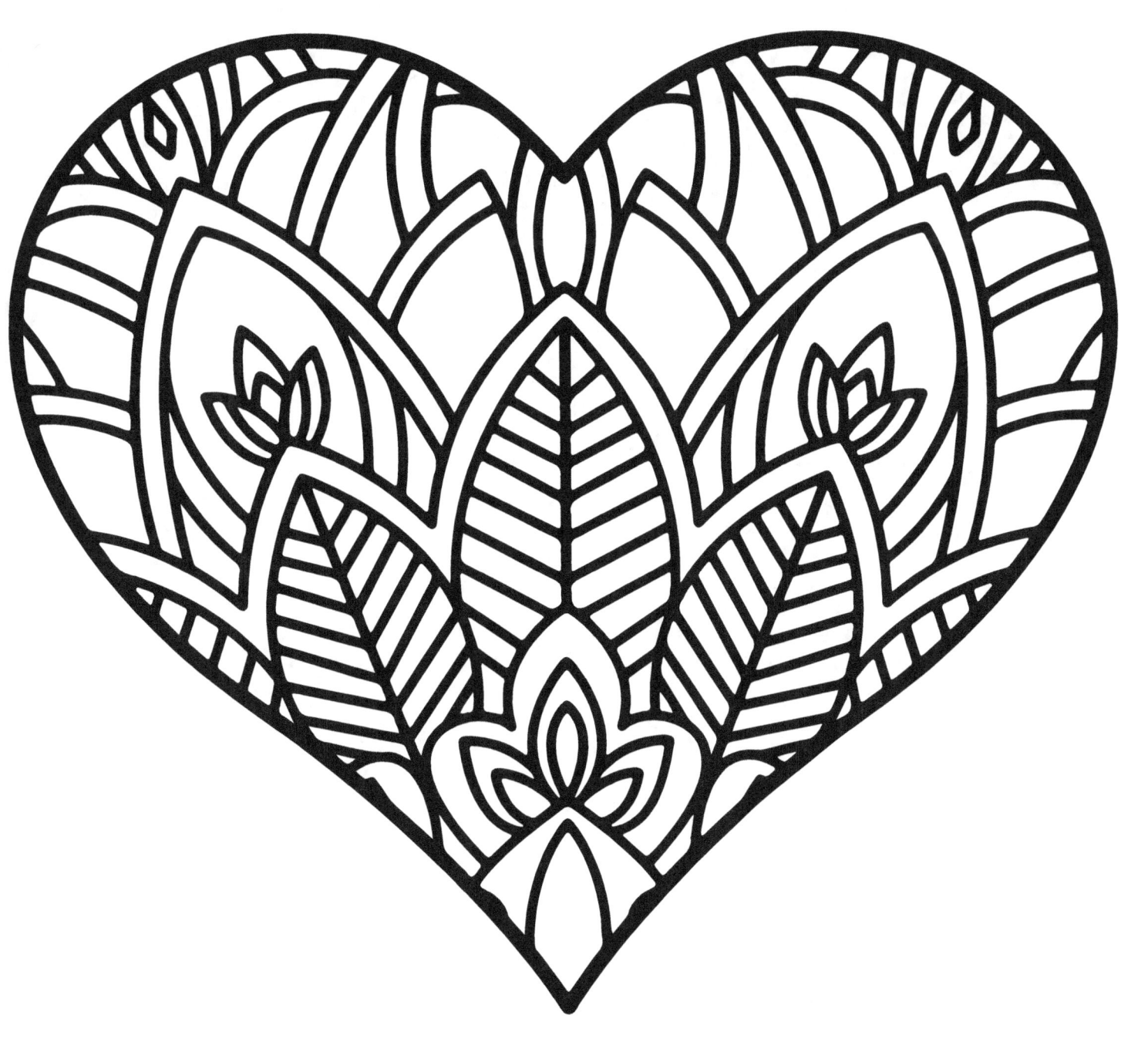

Mandala Hearts

by Little Mary

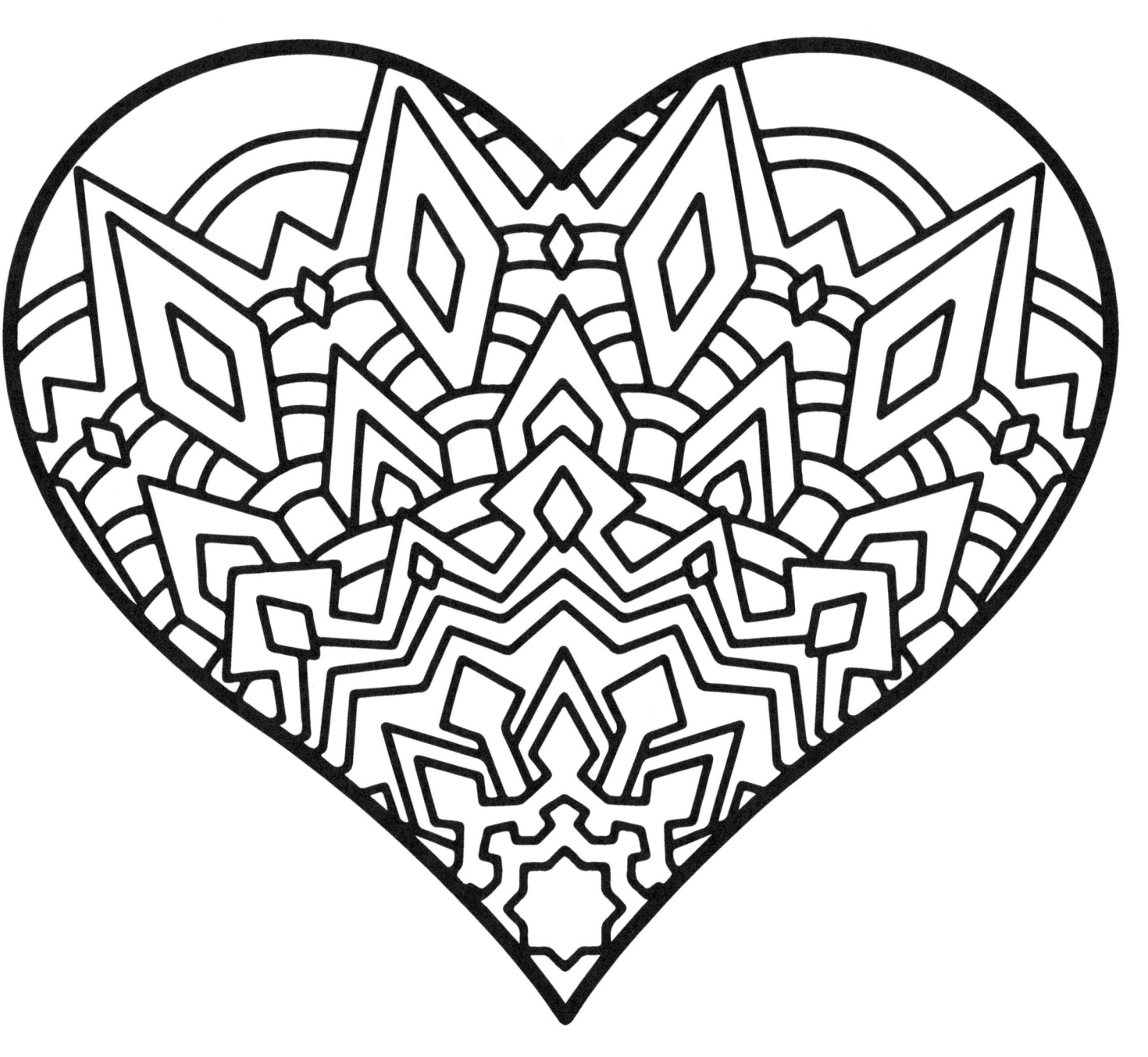

MANDALA HEARTS

by Little Mary

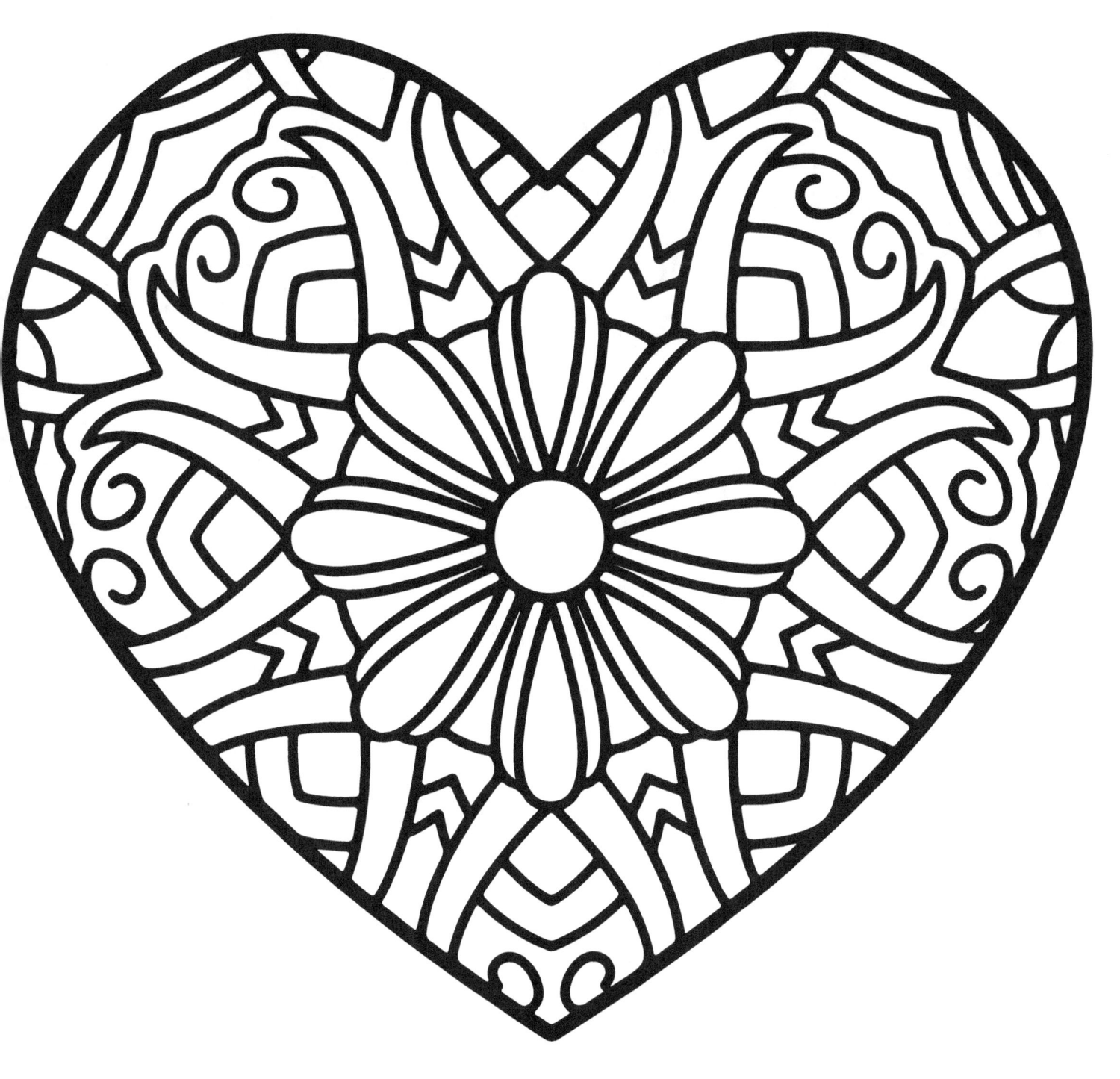

MANDALA HEARTS

by Little Mary

Mandala Hearts

by Little Mary

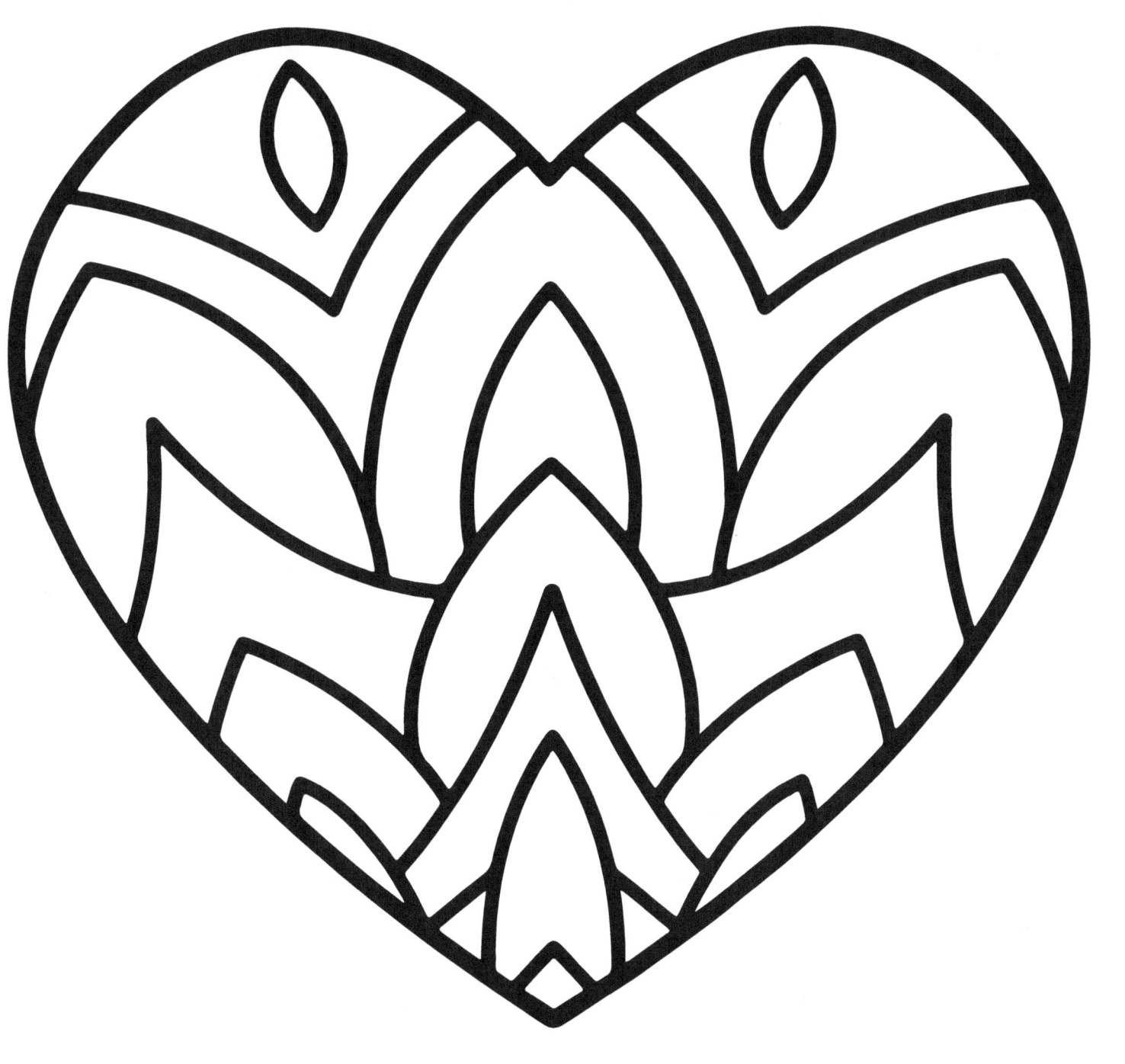

MANDALA HEARTS

by Little Mary

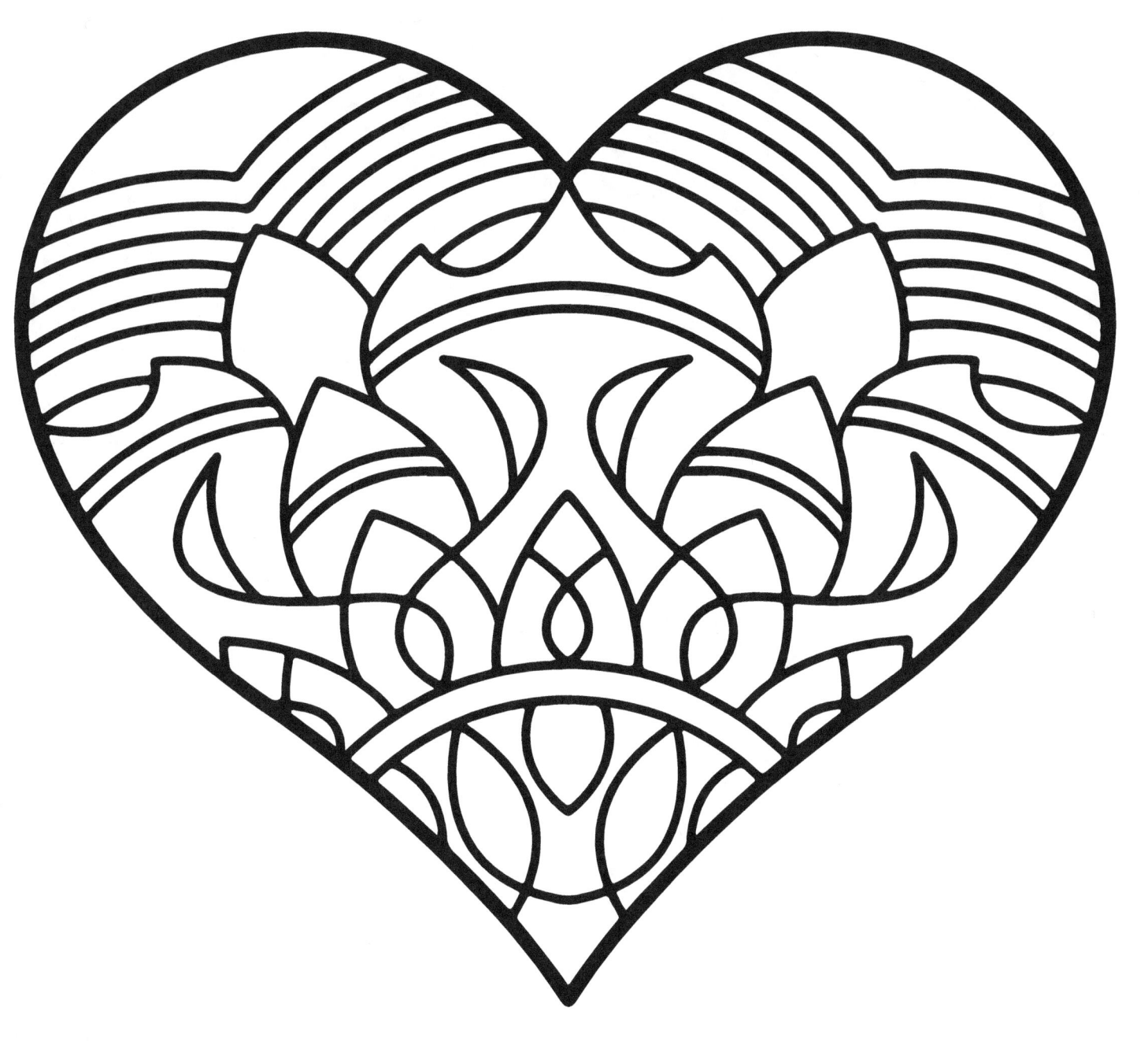

Mandala Hearts

by Little Mary

MANDALA HEARTS

by Little Mary

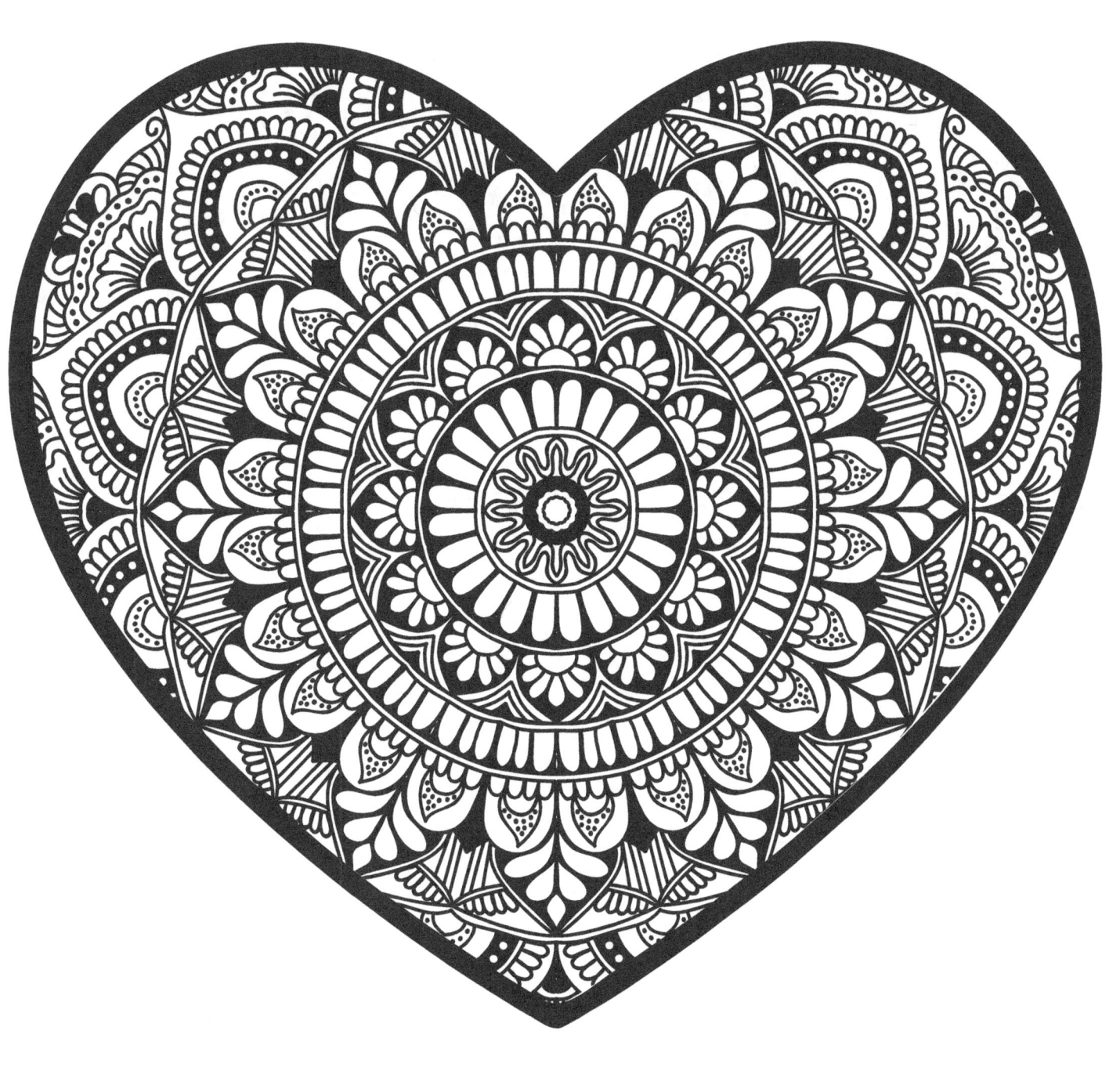

MANDALA HEARTS

by Little Mary

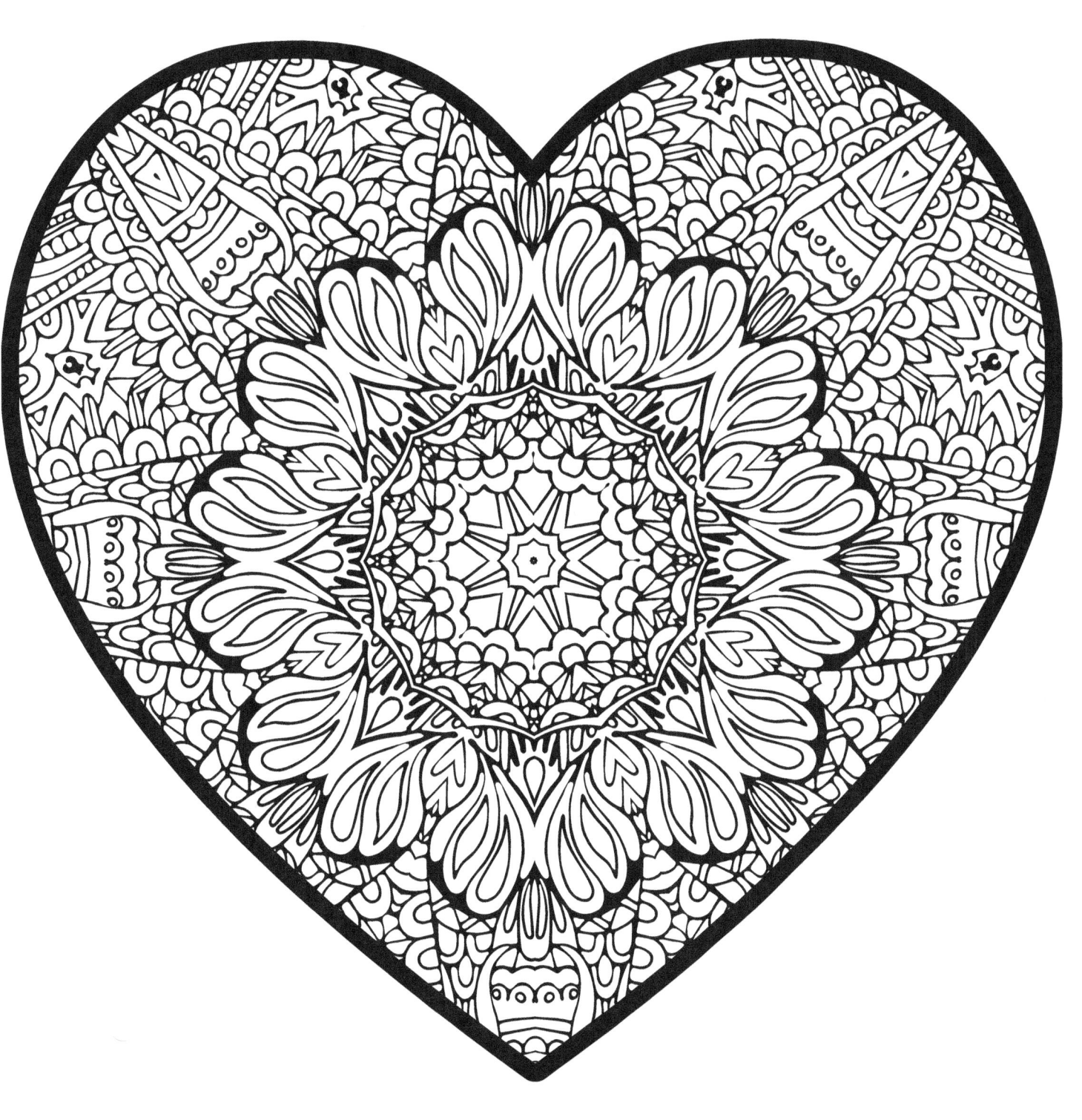

MANDALA HEARTS

by Little Mary

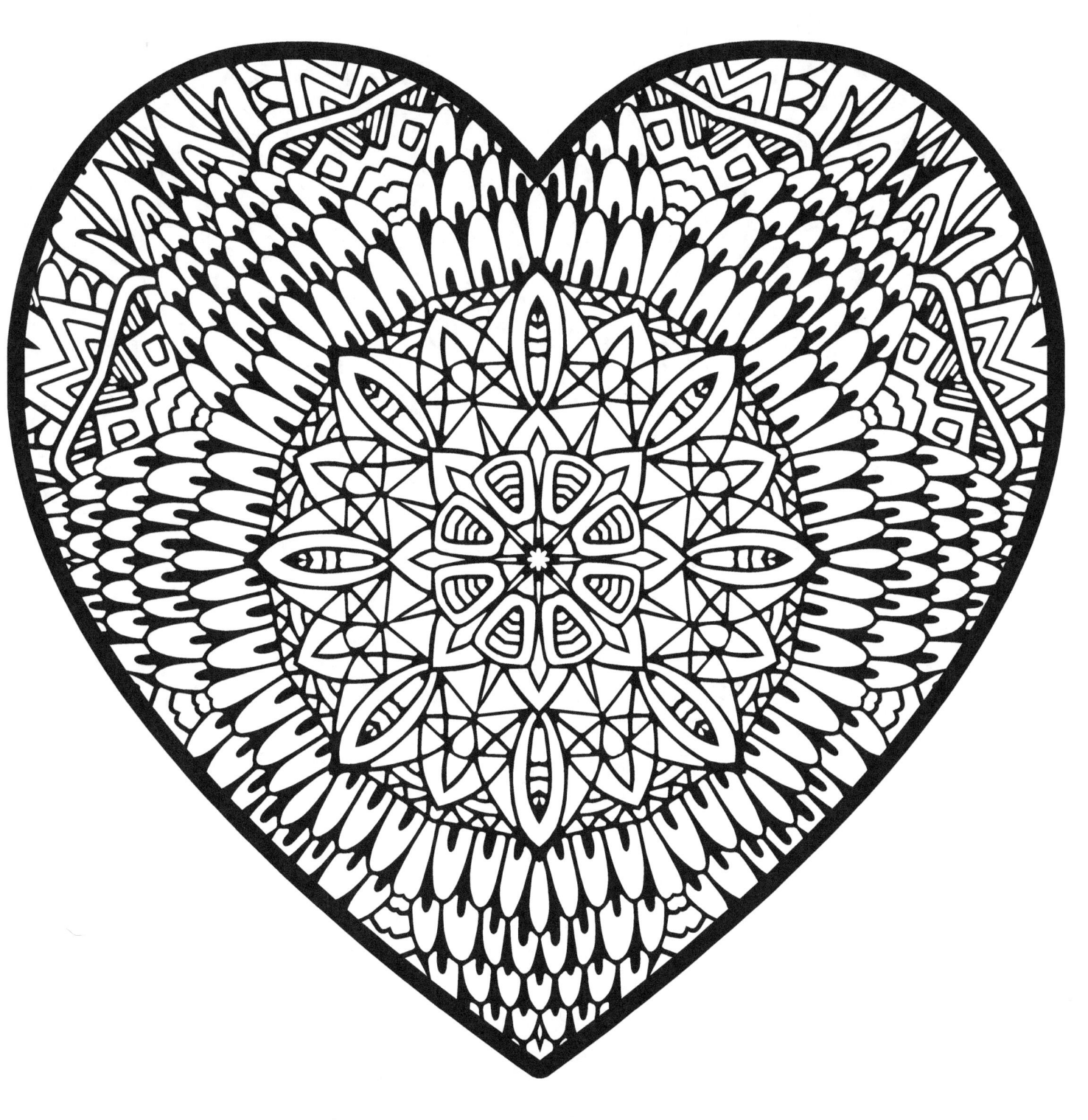

MANDALA HEARTS

by Little Mary

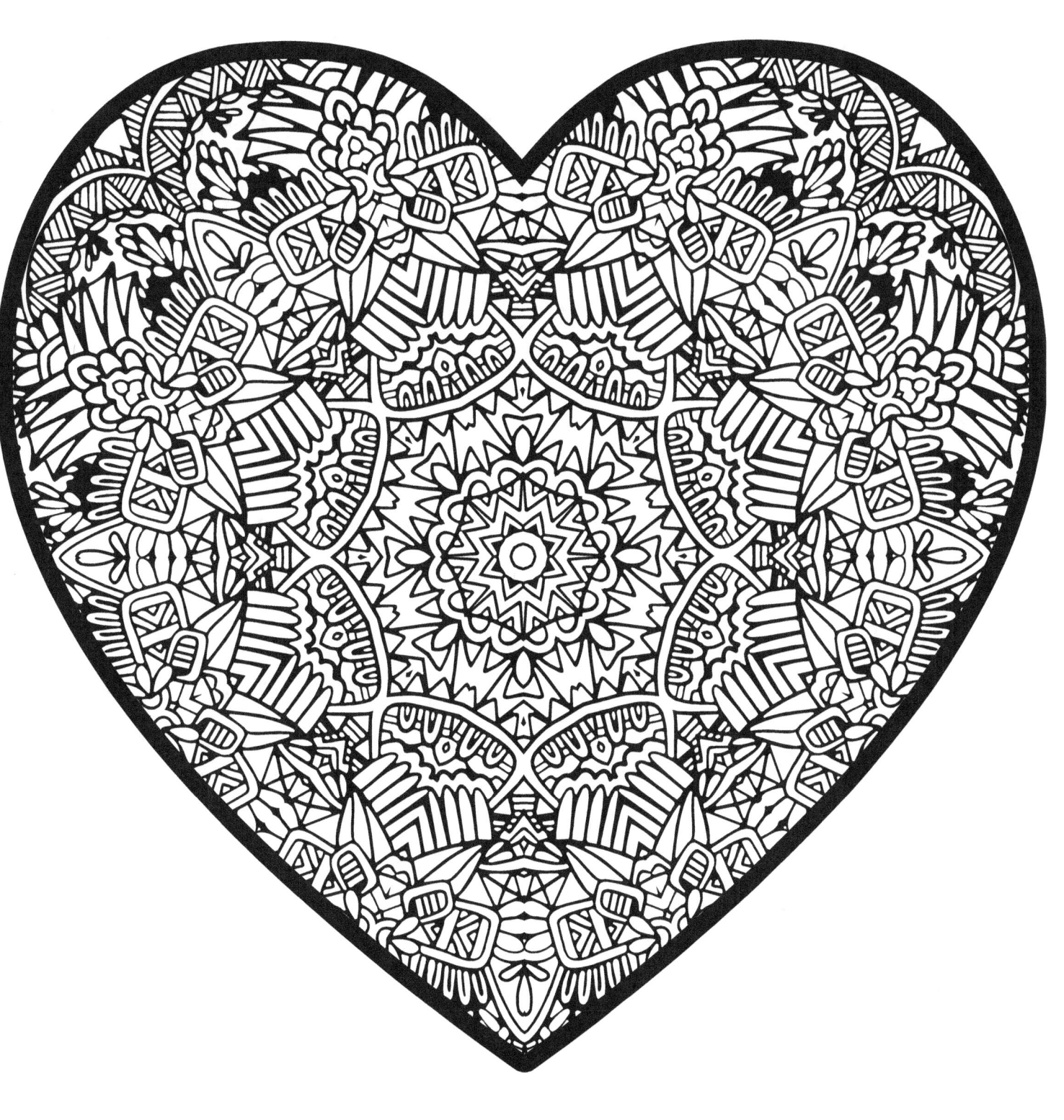

Mandala Hearts

by Little Mary

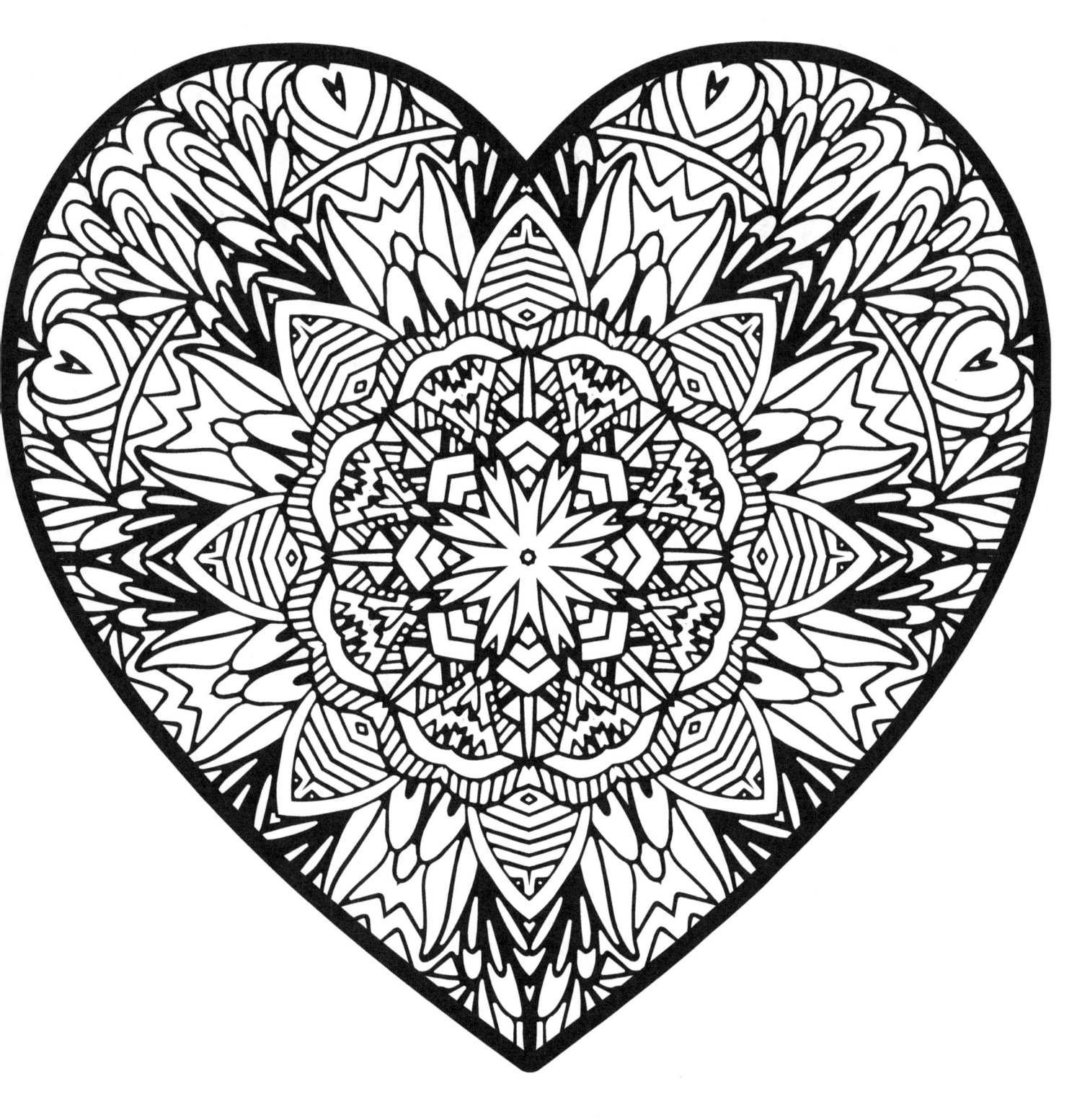

Mandala Hearts

by Little Mary

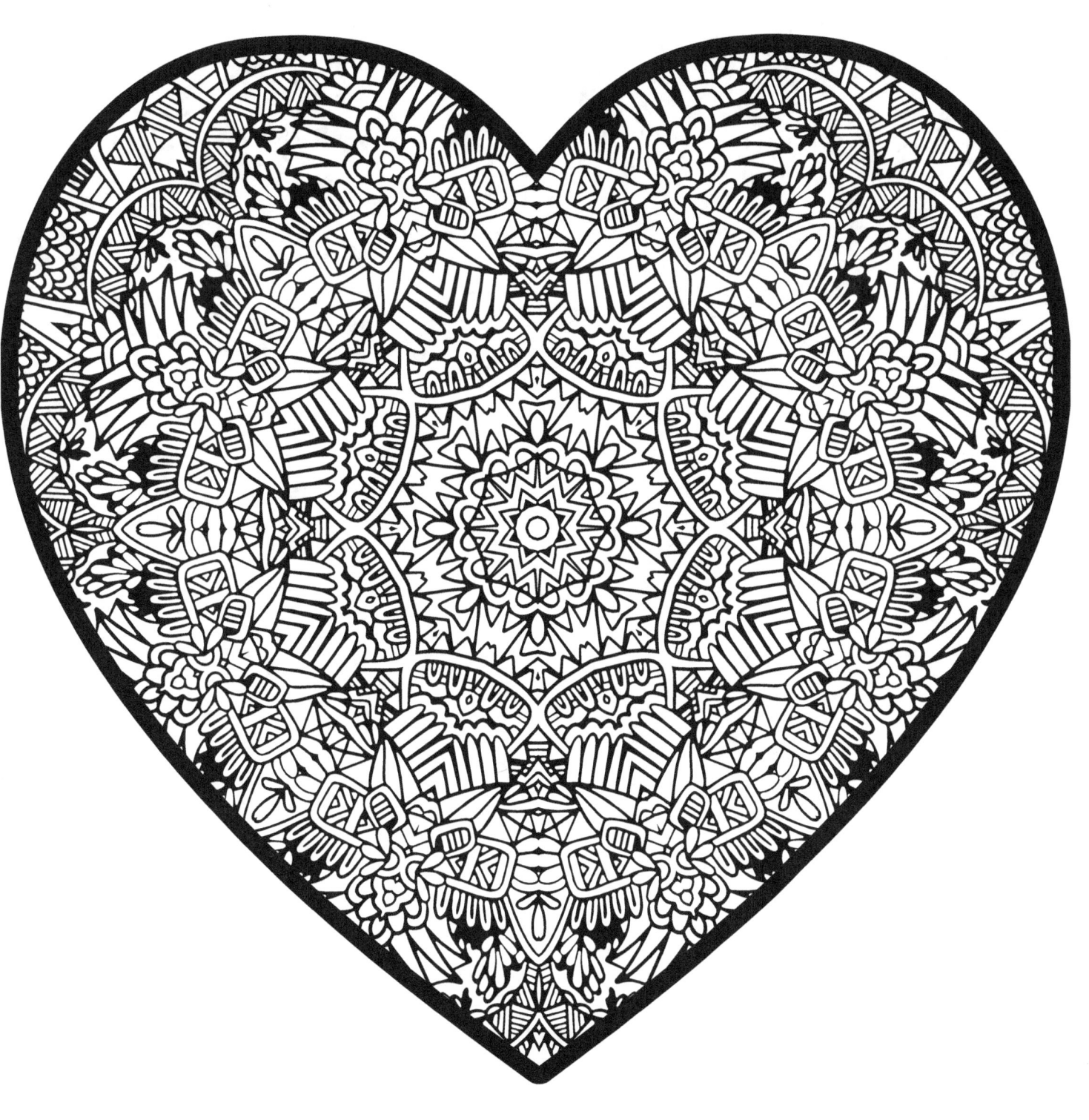

Mandala Hearts

by Little Mary

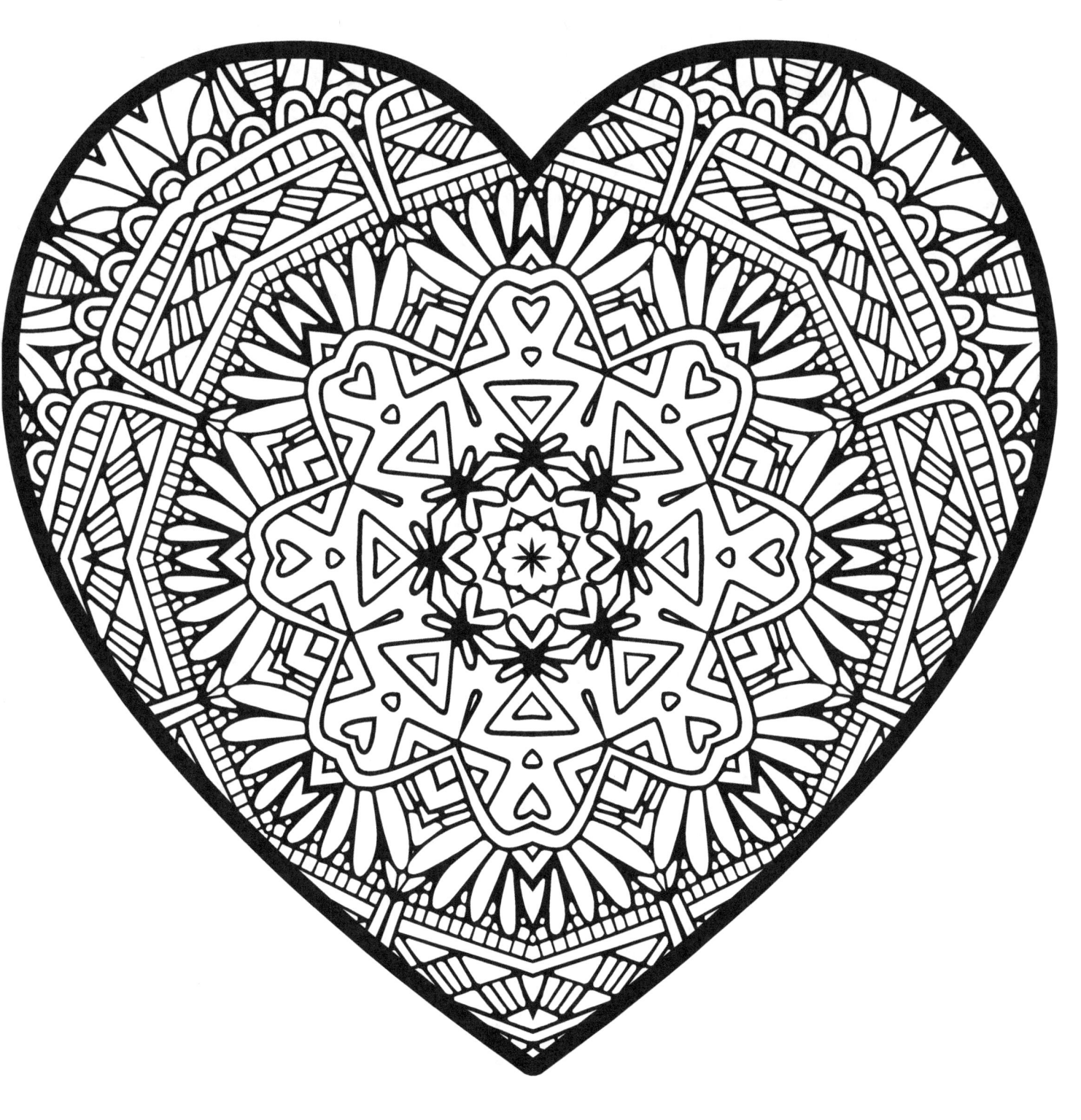

Mandala Hearts

by Little Mary

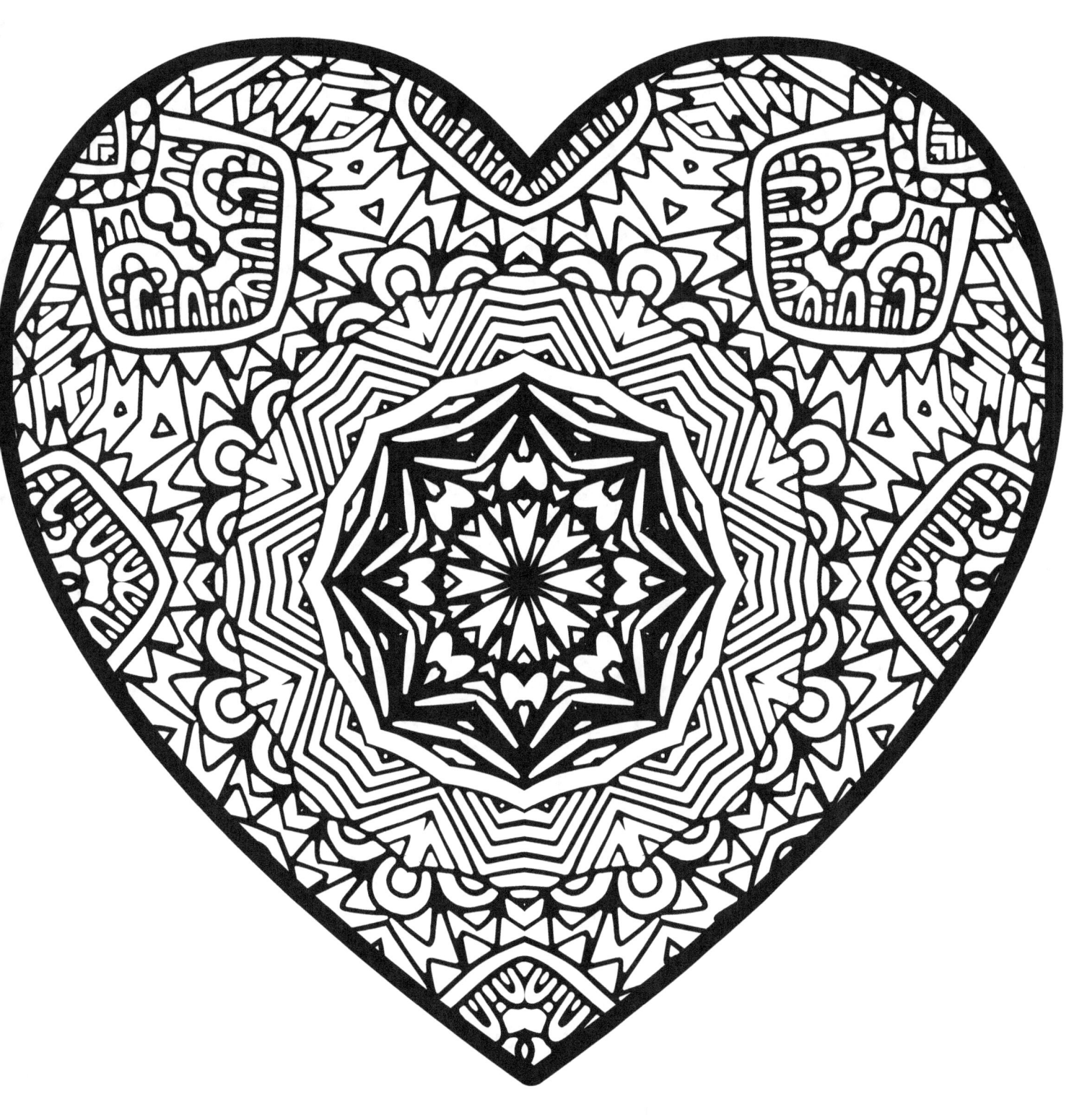

MANDALA HEARTS

by Little Mary

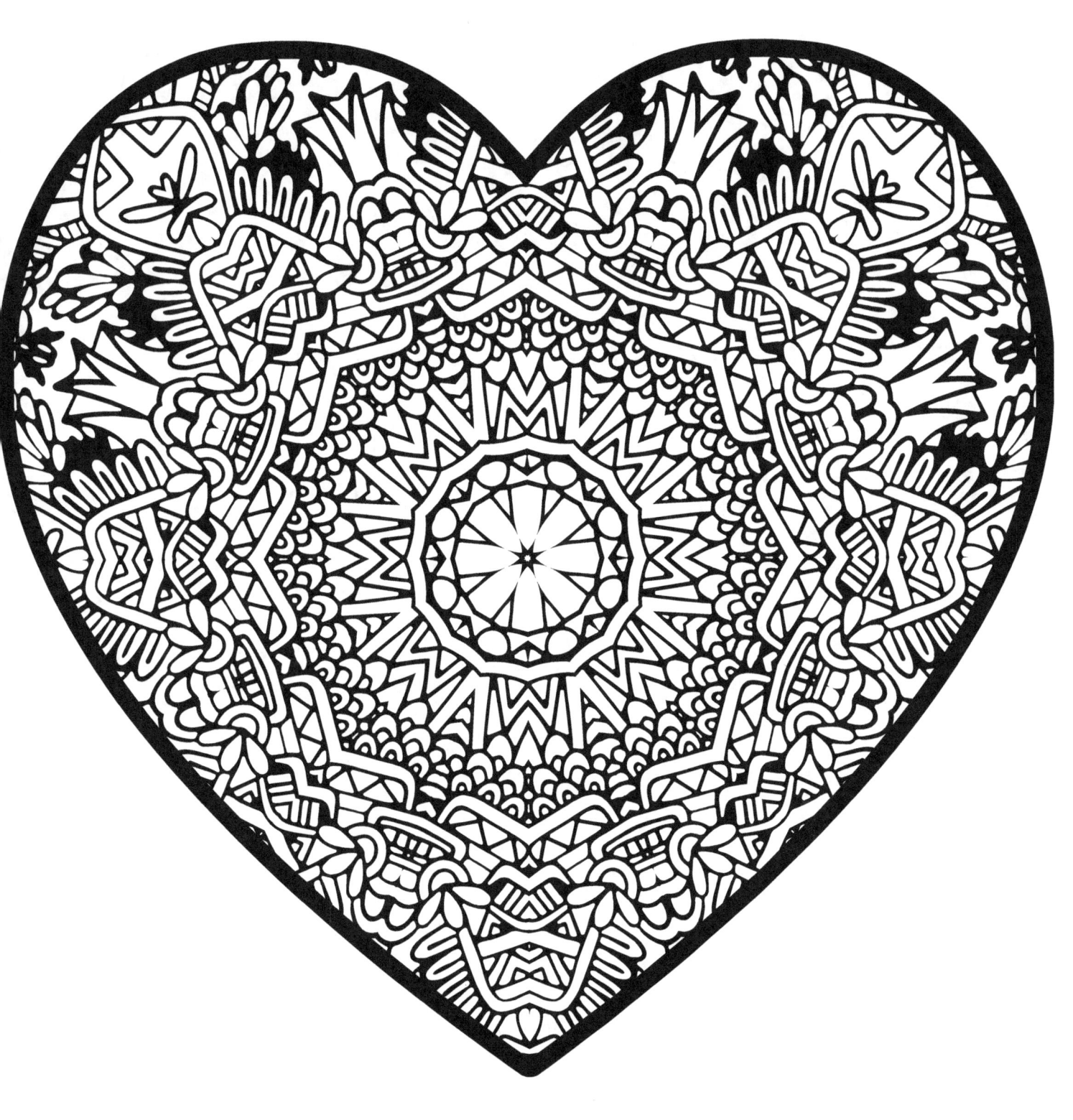

MANDALA HEARTS

by Little Mary

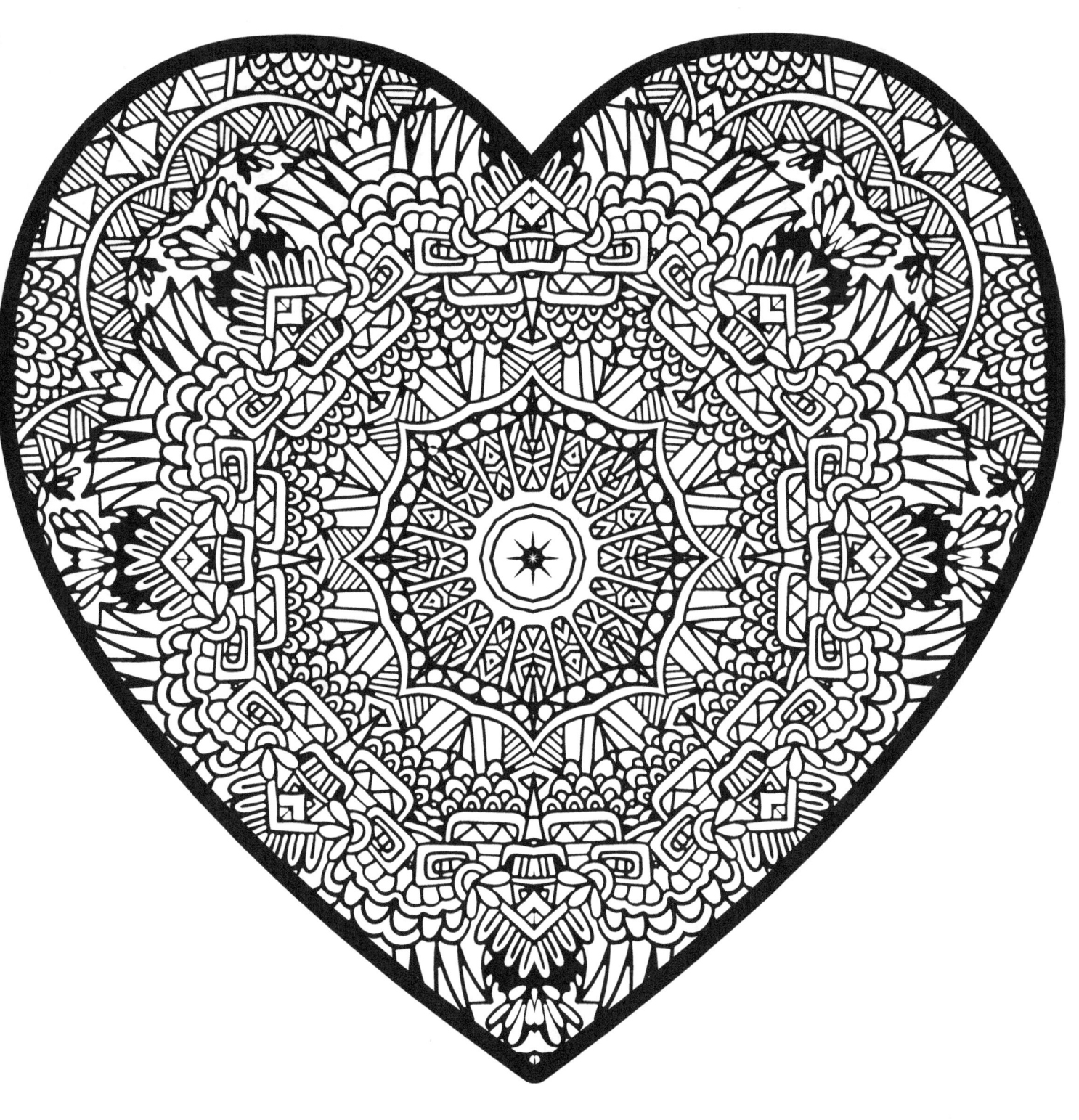

MANDALA HEARTS

by Little Mary

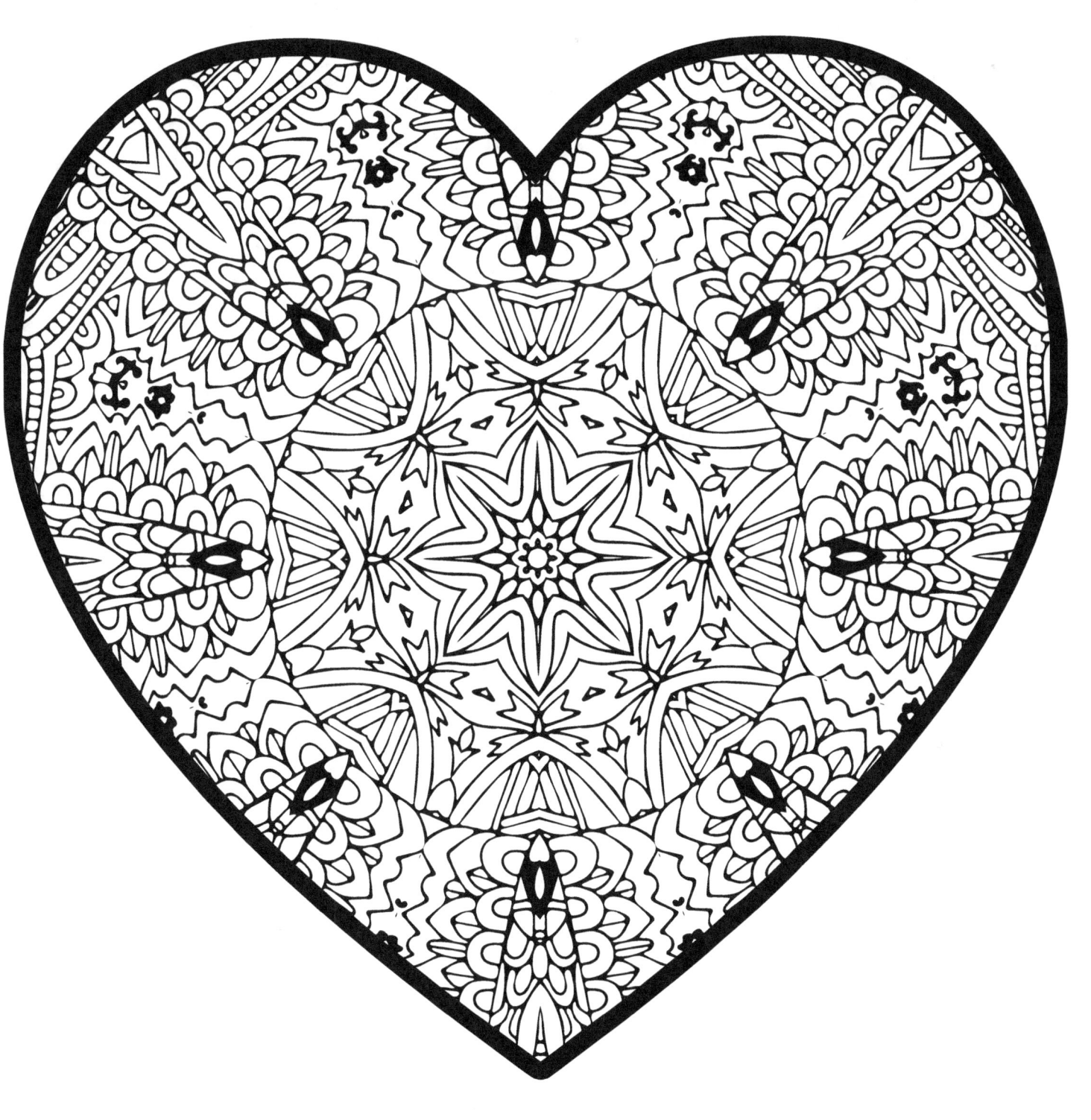

MANDALA HEARTS

by Little Mary

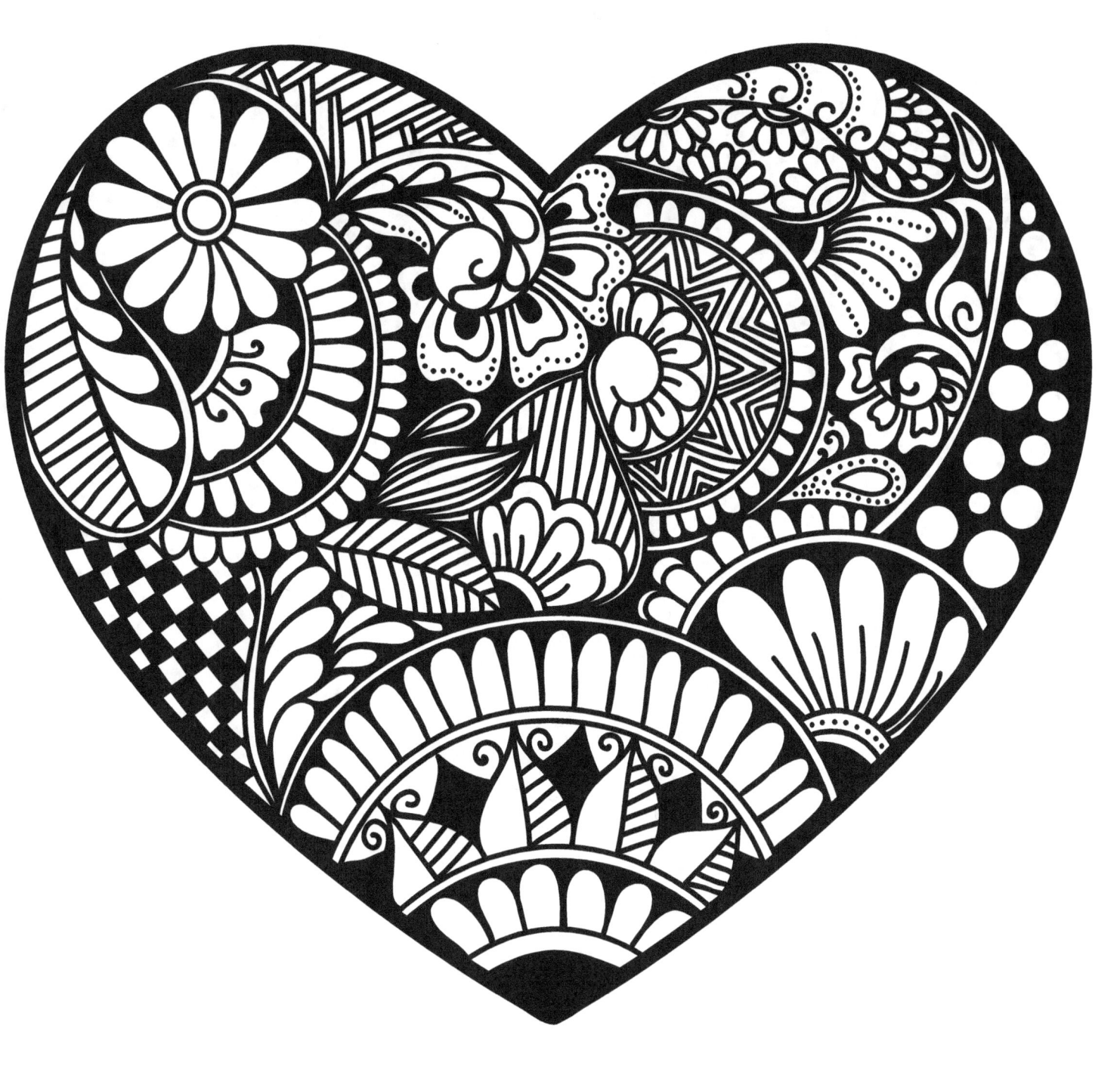

Mandala Hearts

by Little Mary

MANDALA HEARTS

by Little Mary

Mandala Hearts

by Little Mary

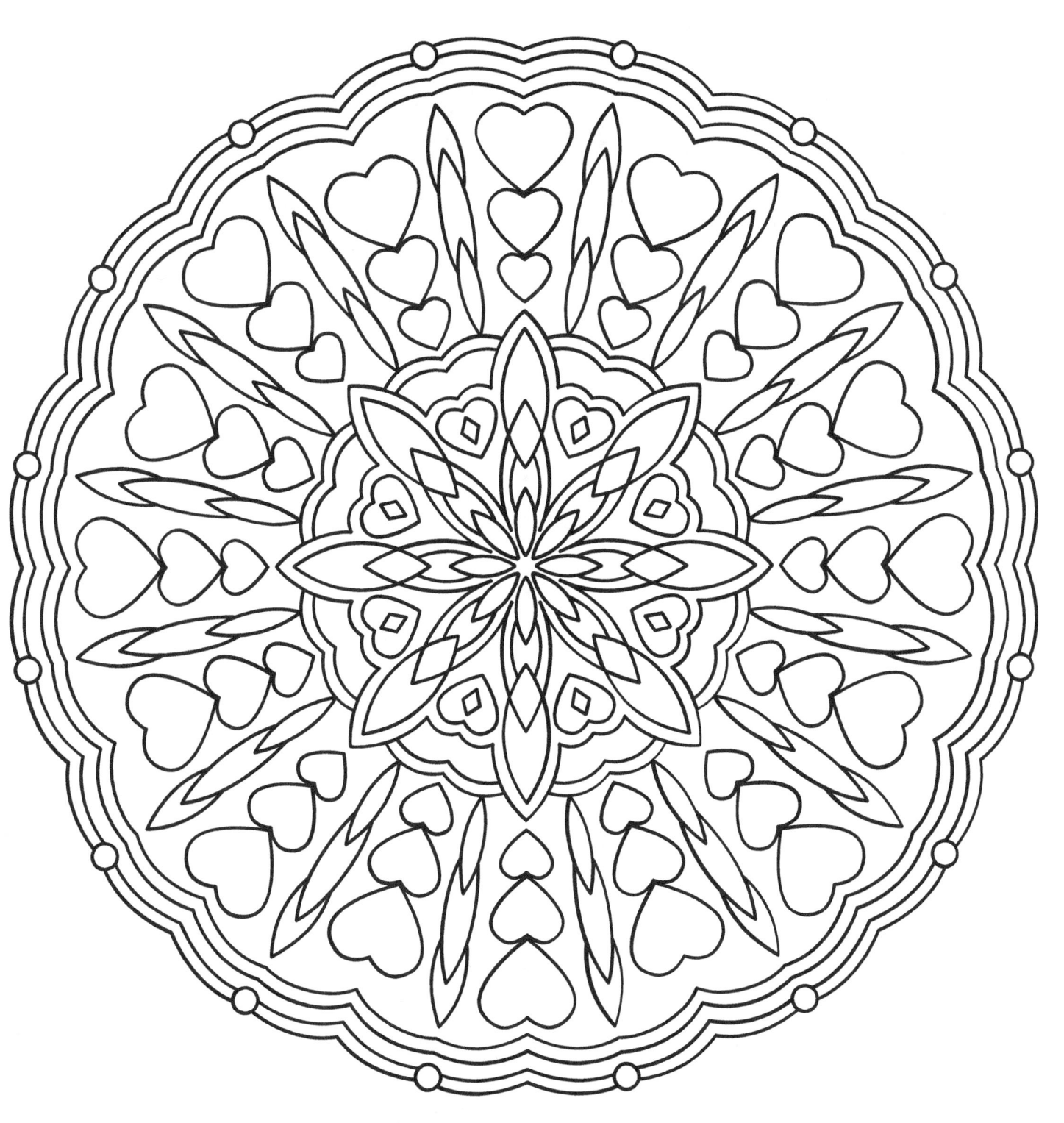

Mandala Hearts

by Little Mary

Mandala Hearts

by Little Mary

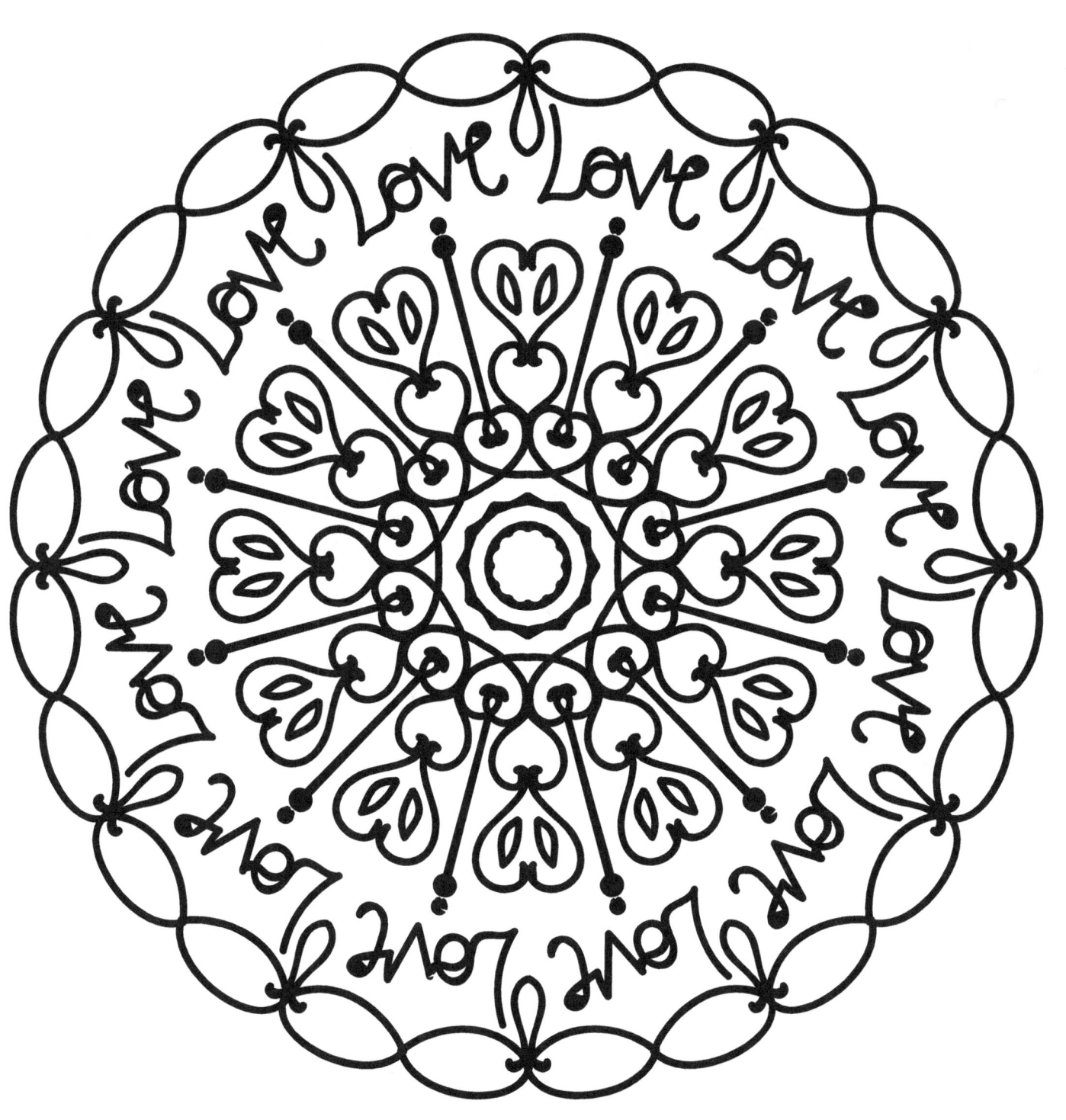

MANDALA HEARTS

by Little Mary

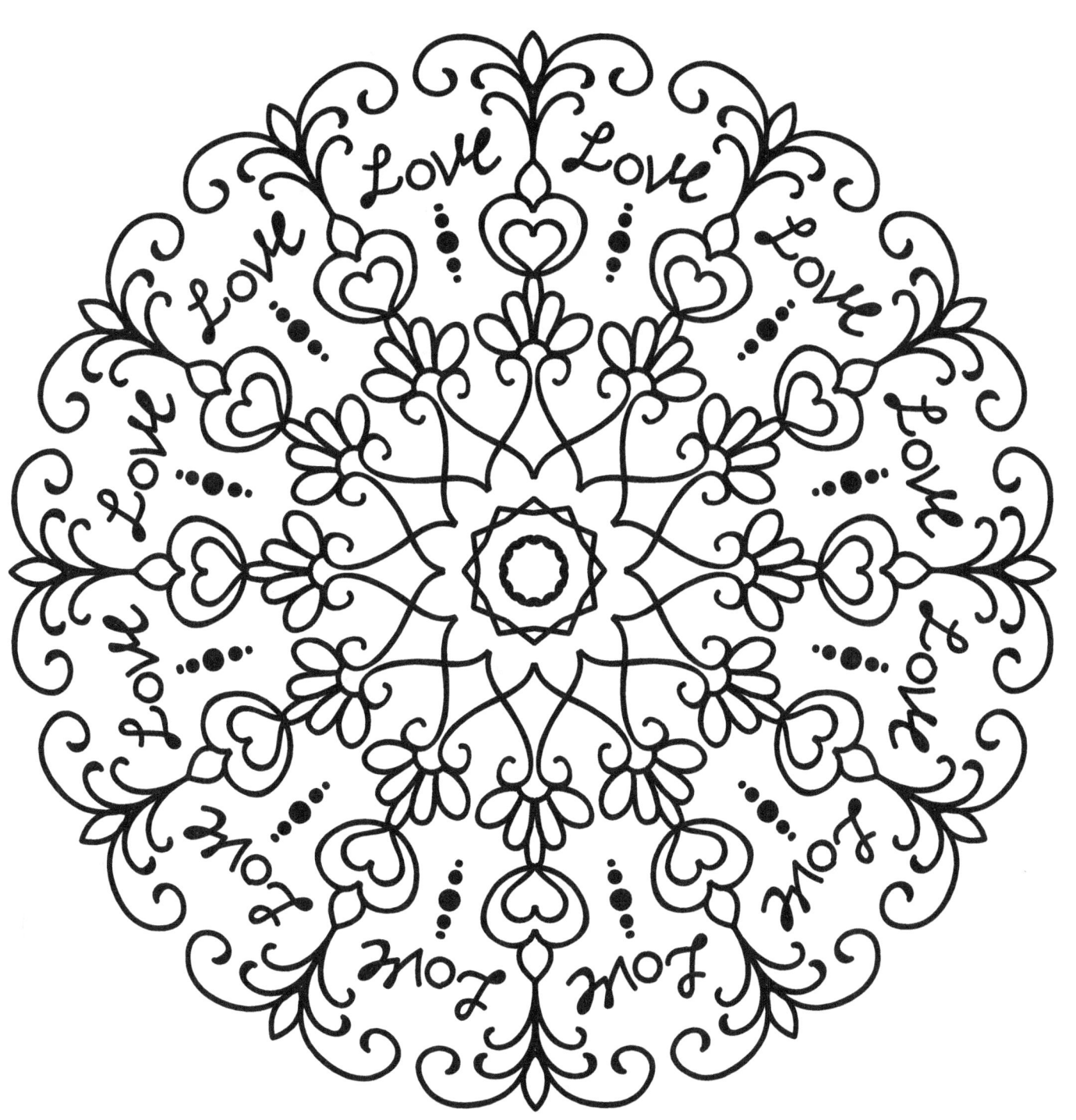

Mandala Hearts

by Little Mary

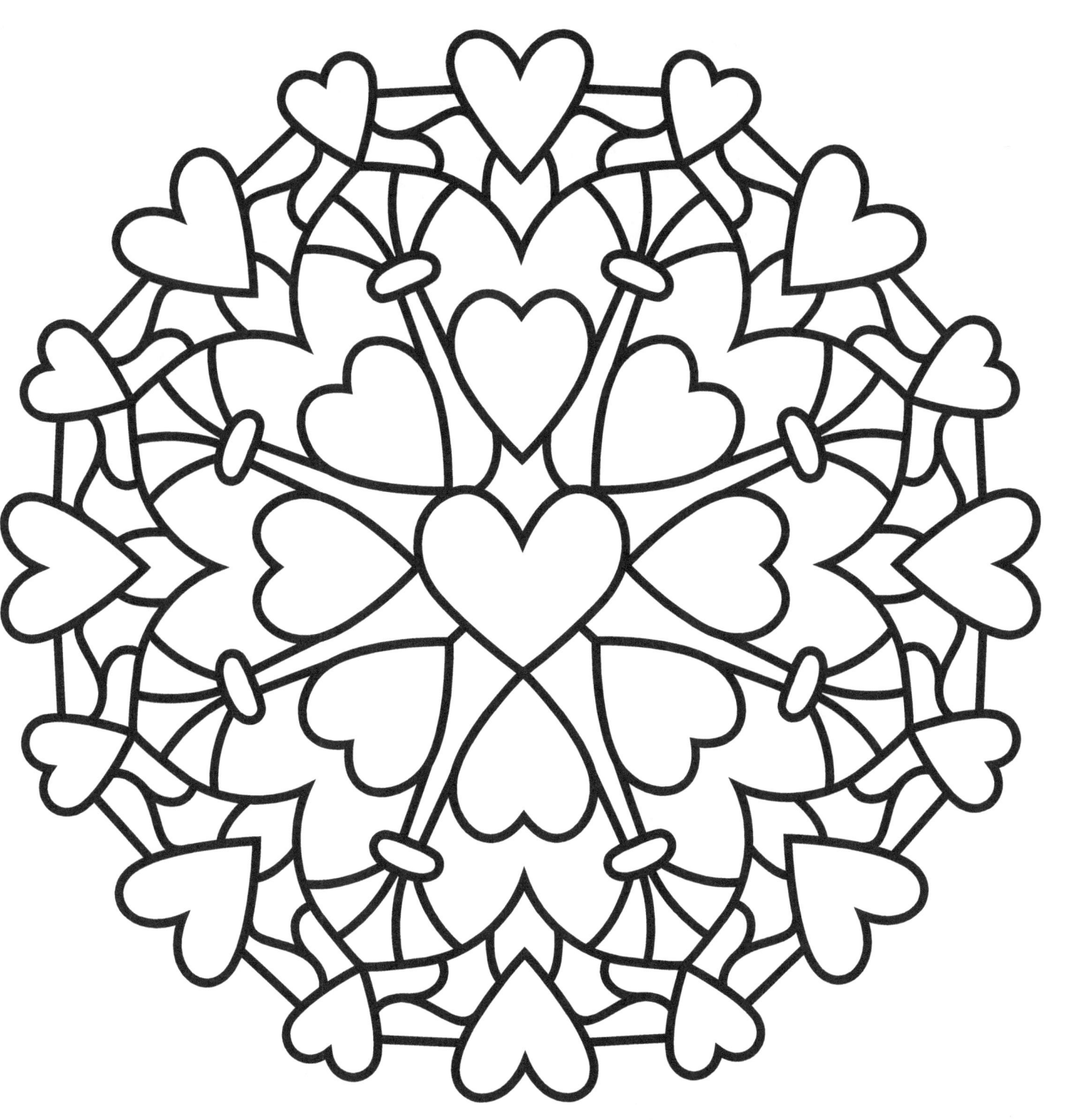

Mandala Hearts

by Little Mary

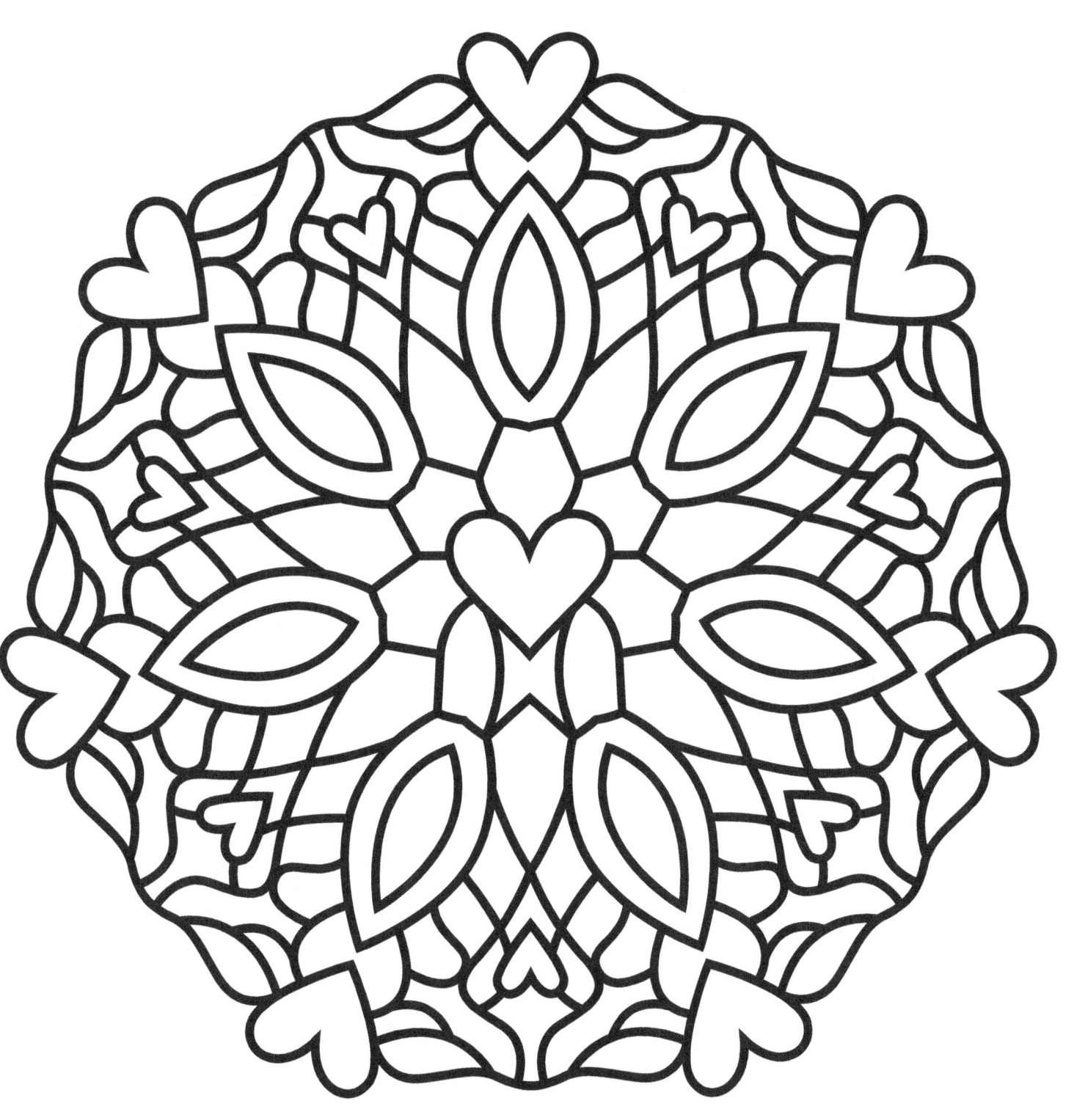

Mandala Hearts

by Little Mary

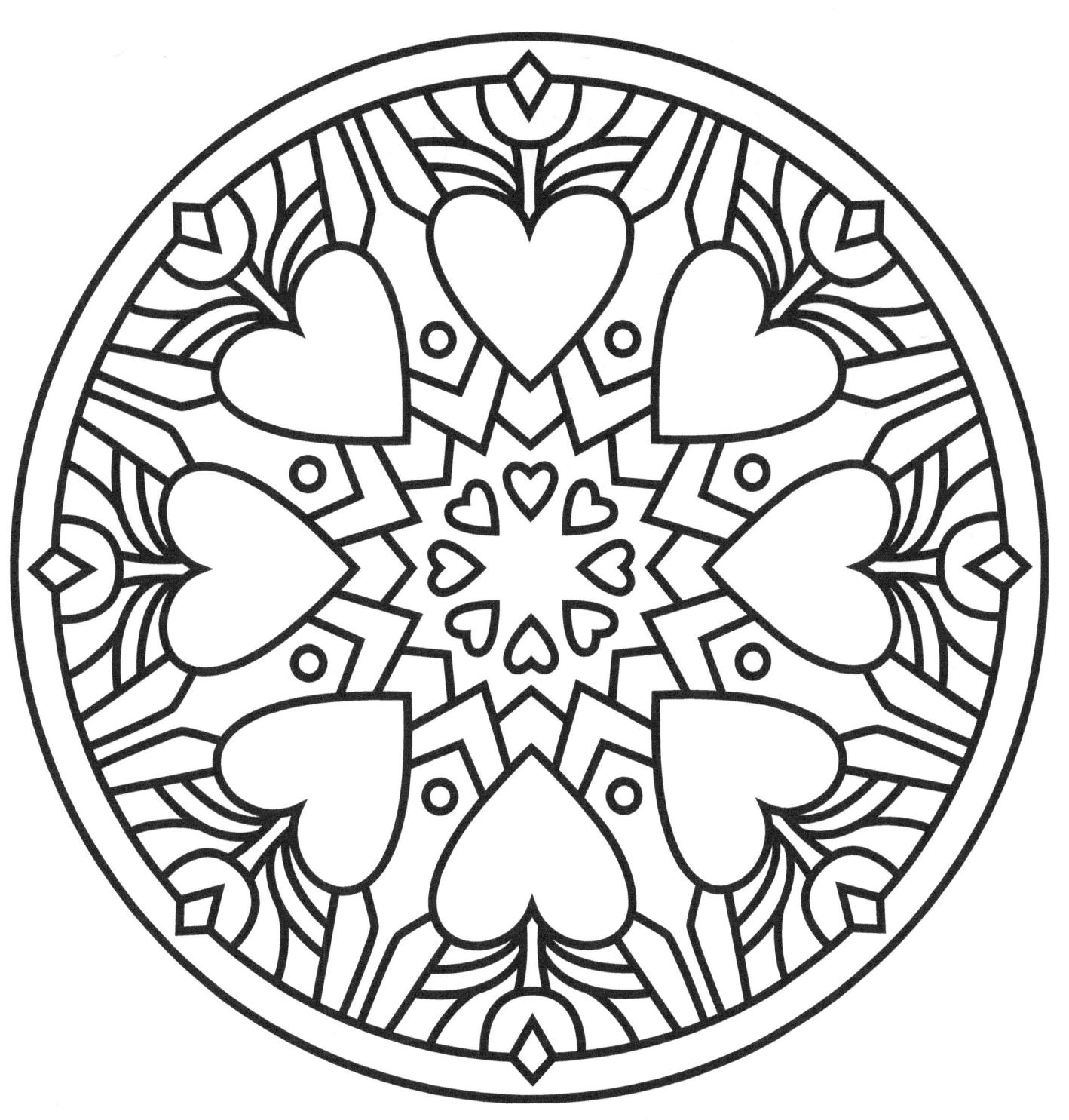

MANDALA HEARTS

by Little Mary

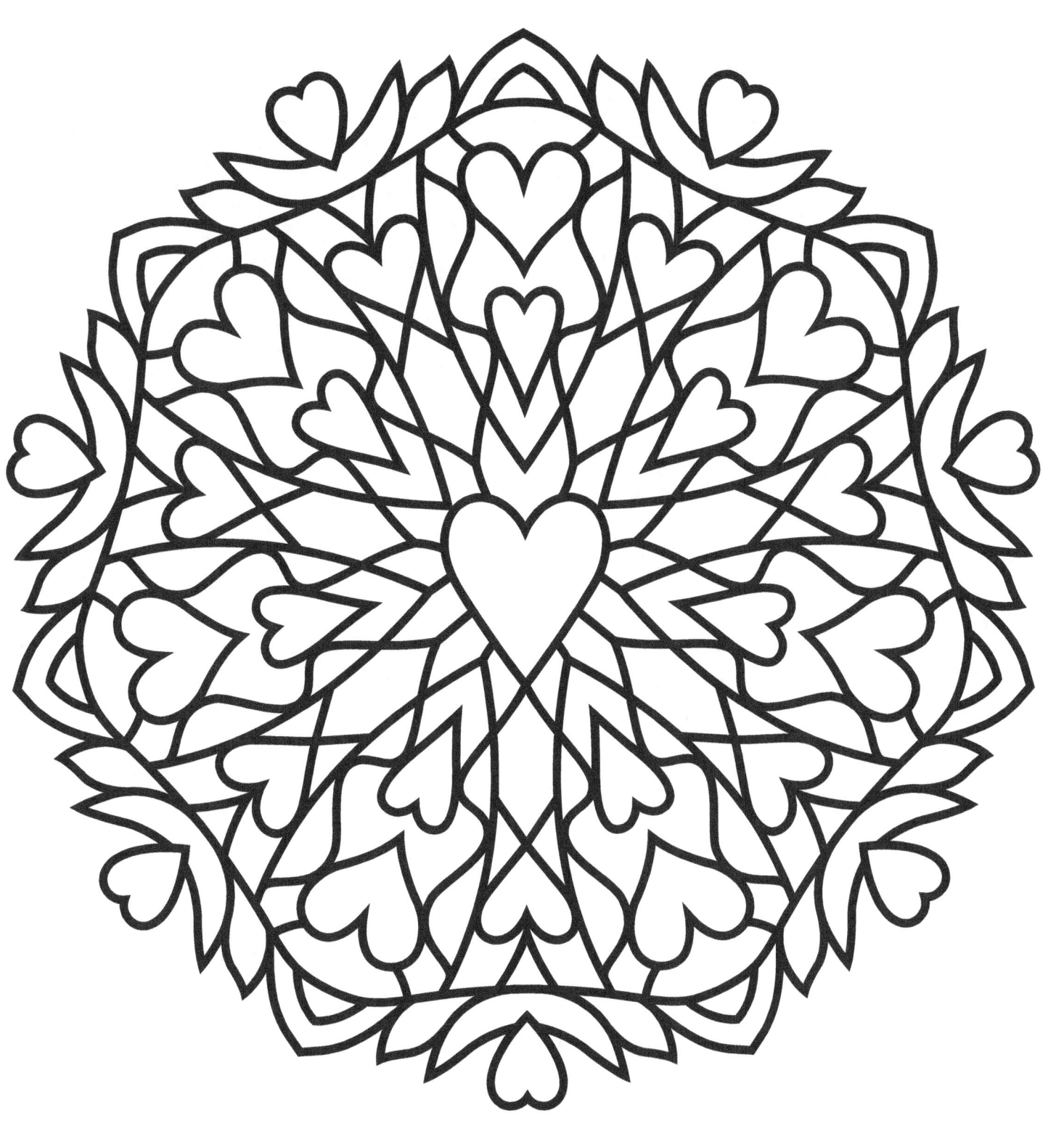

MANDALA HEARTS

by Little Mary

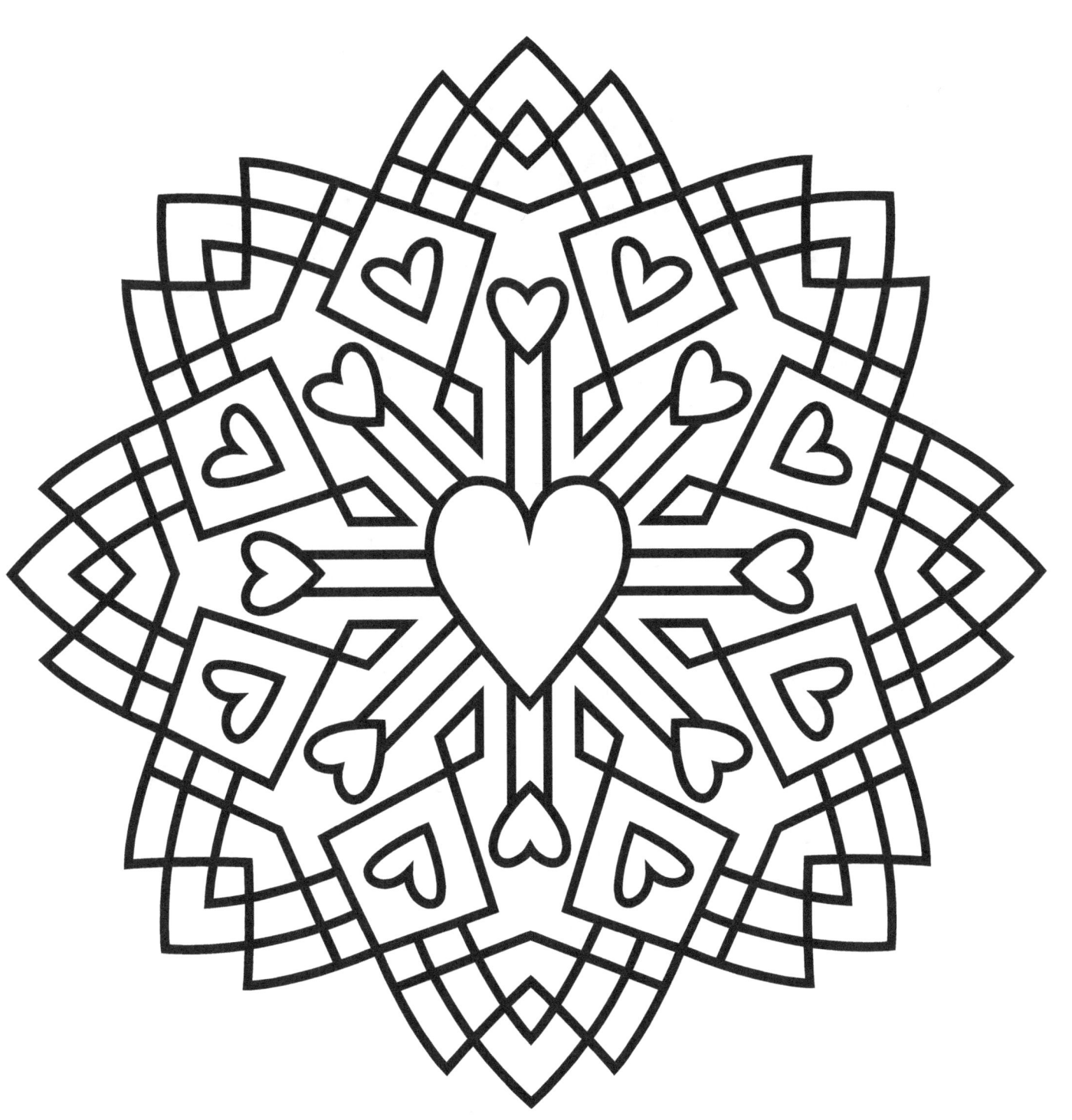

Mandala Hearts

by Little Mary

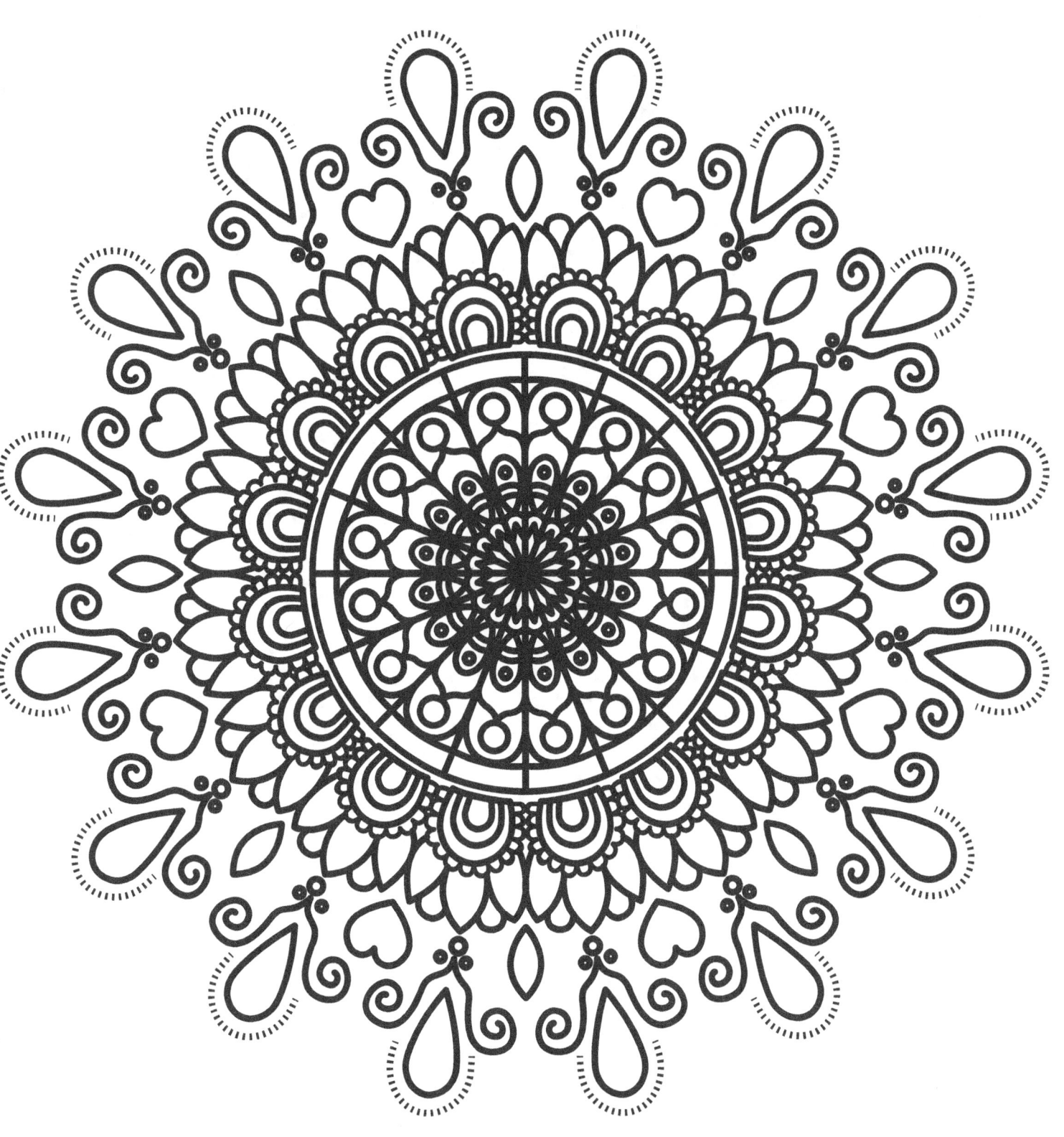

Mandala Hearts

by Little Mary

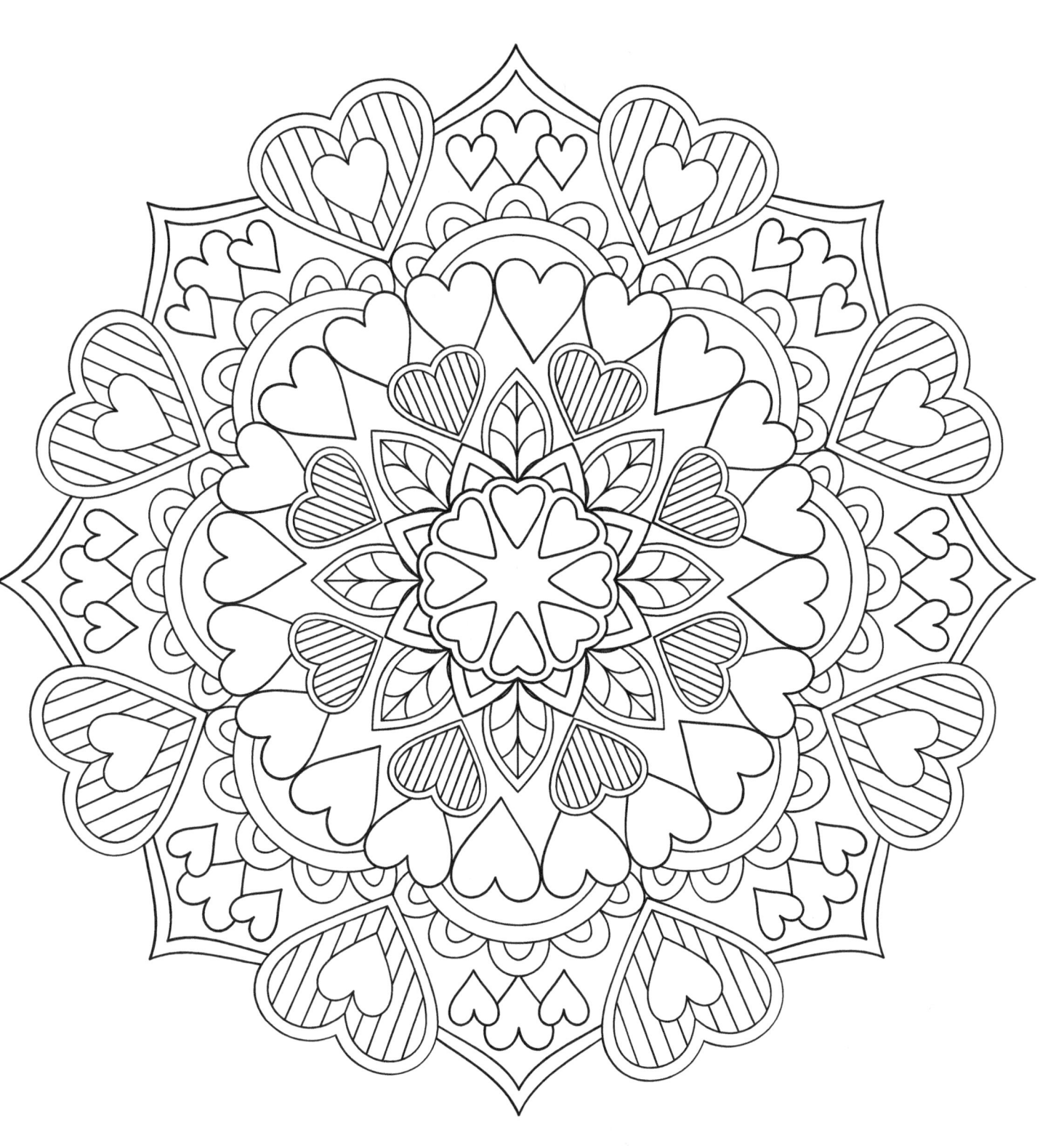

Mandala Hearts

by Little Mary

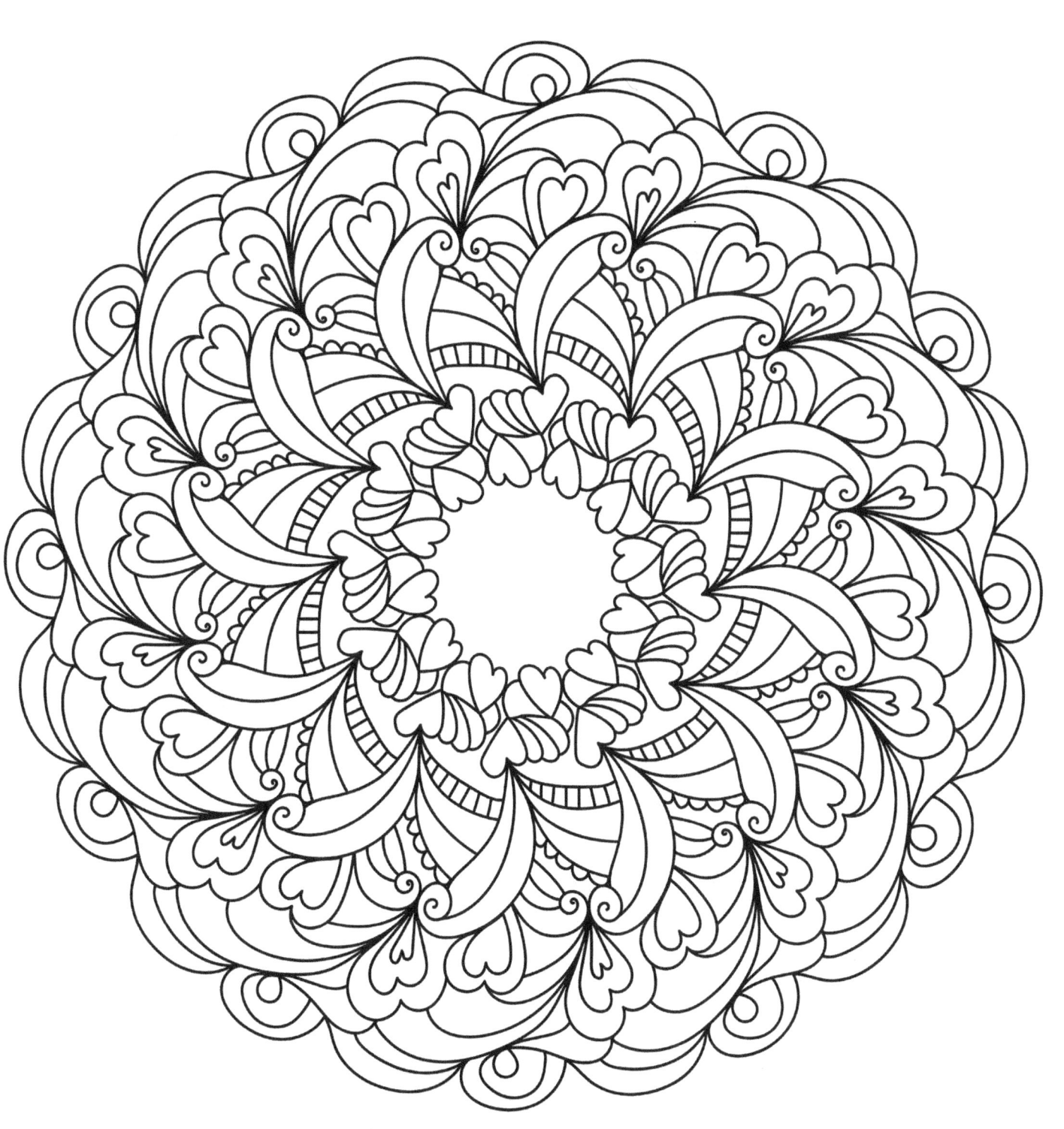

MANDALA HEARTS

by Little Mary

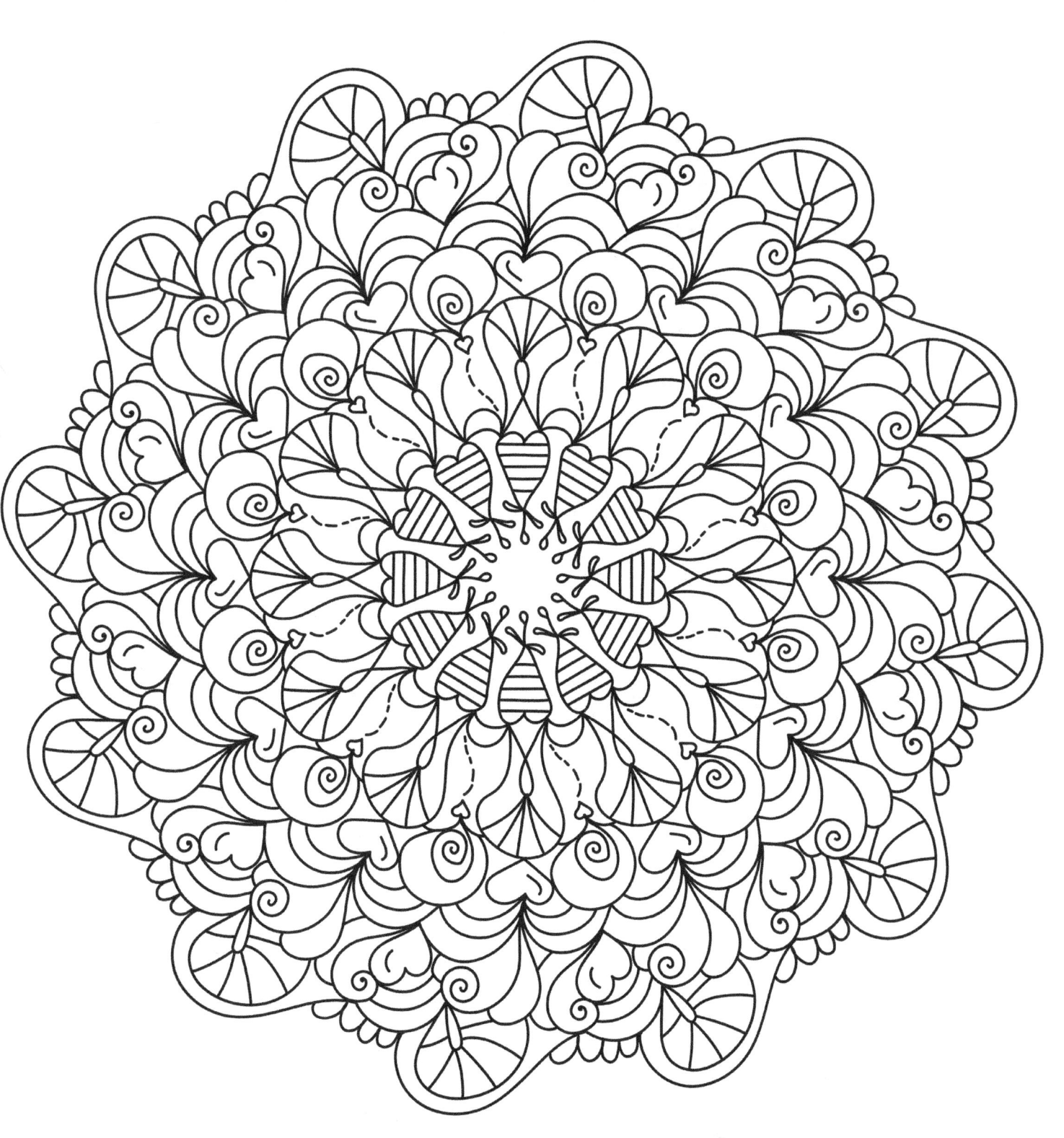

Mandala Hearts

by Little Mary

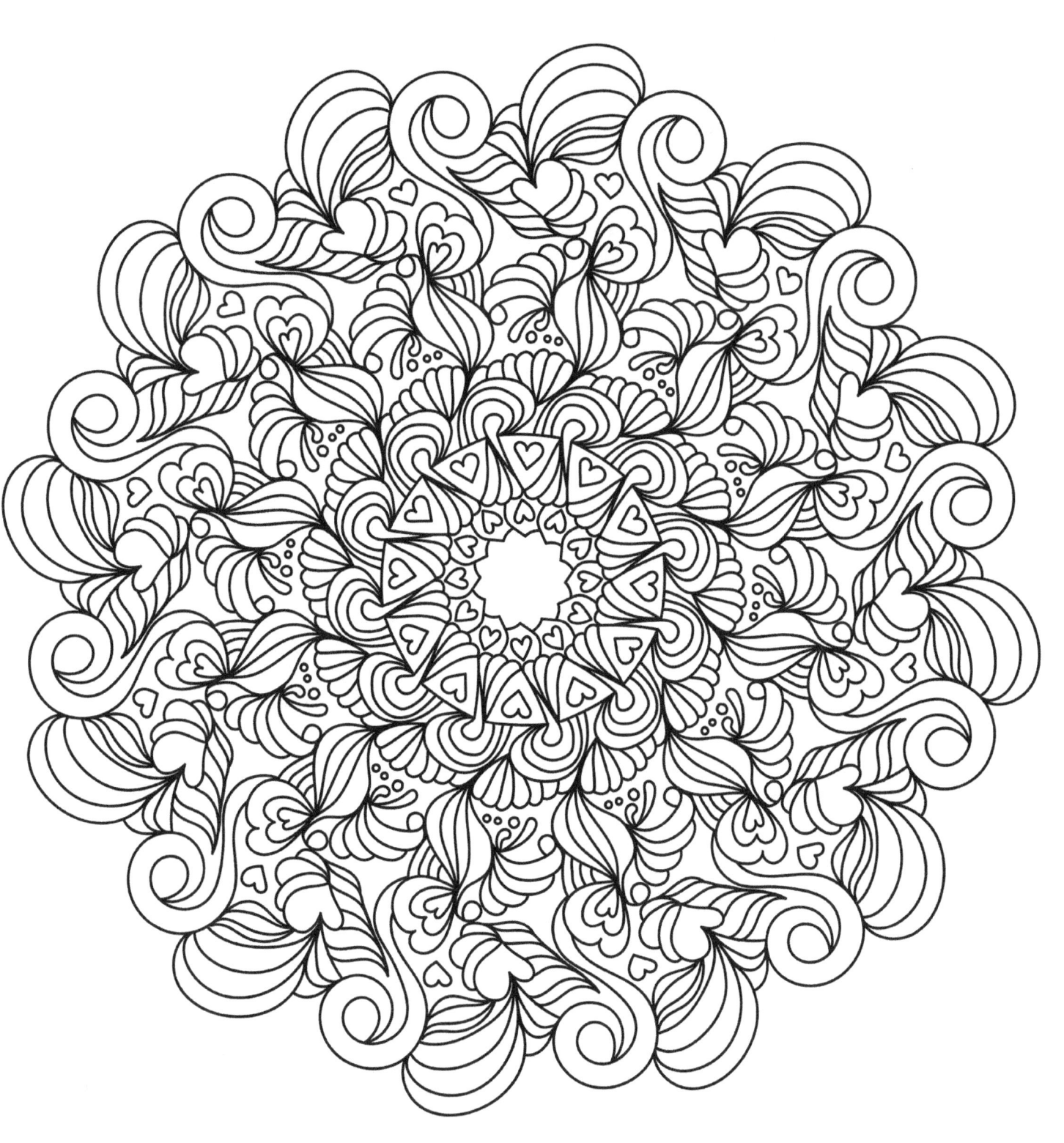

MANDALA HEARTS

by Little Mary

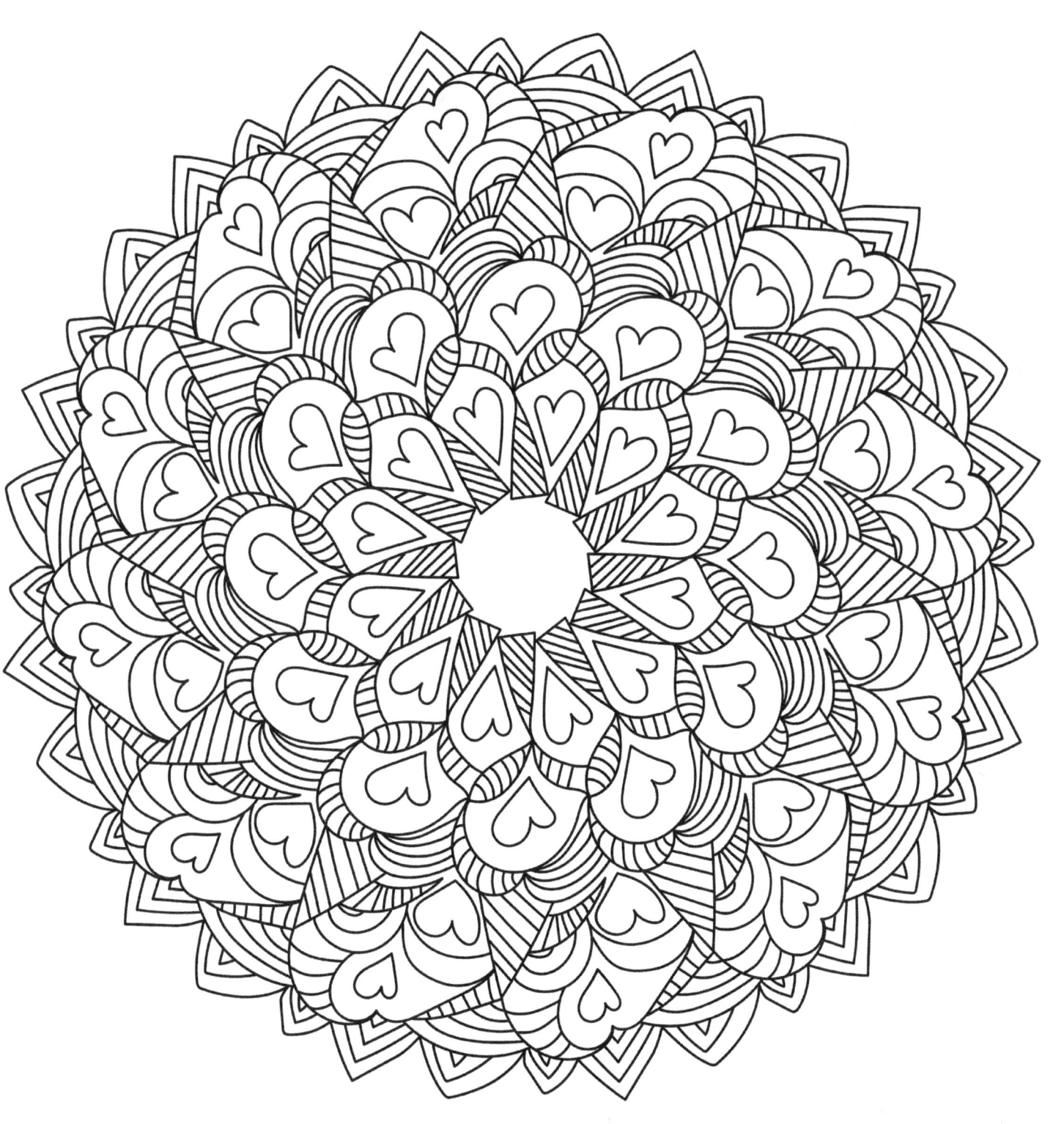

MANDALA HEARTS

by Little Mary

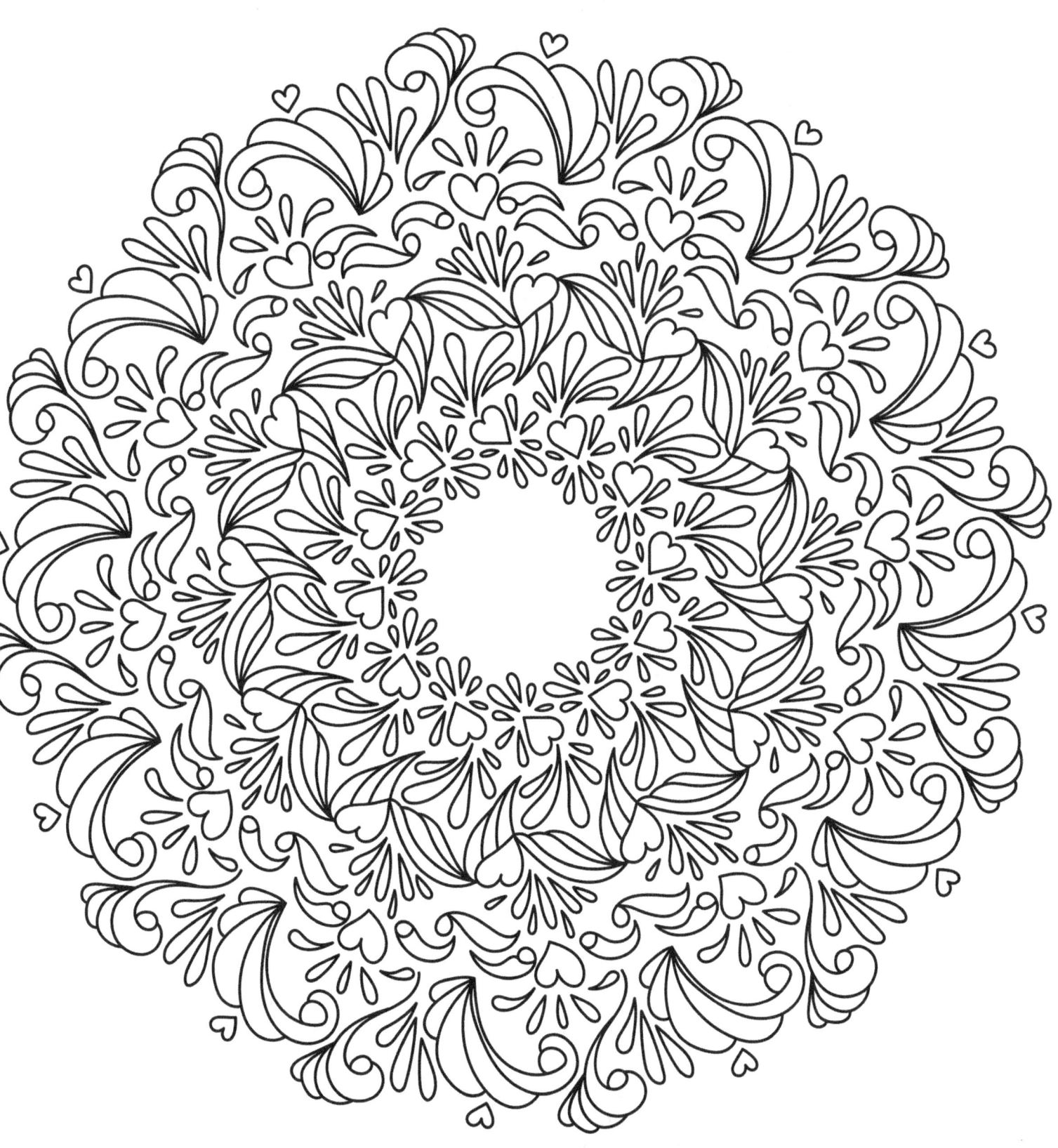

Mandala Hearts

by Little Mary

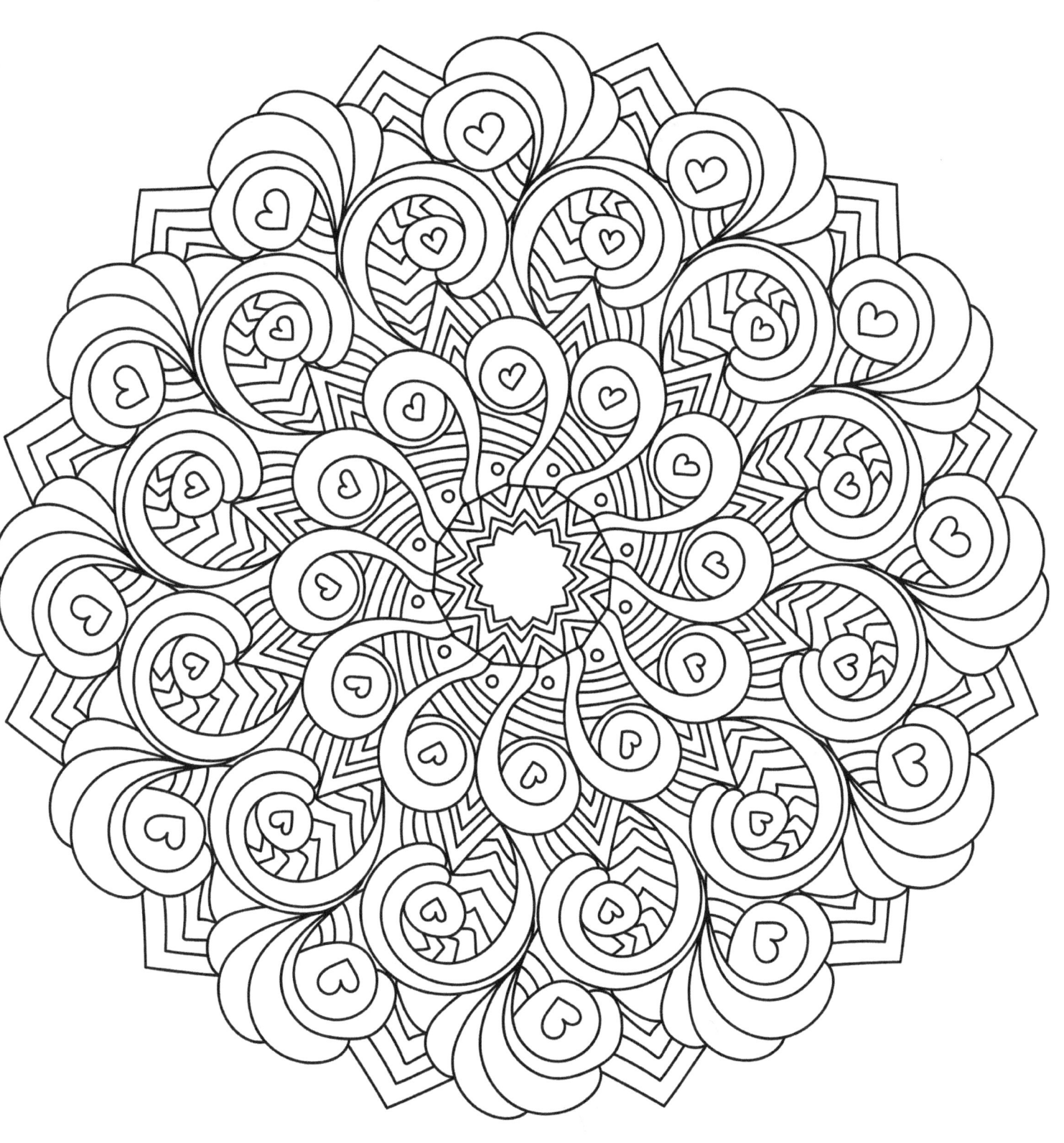

Mandala Hearts

by Little Mary

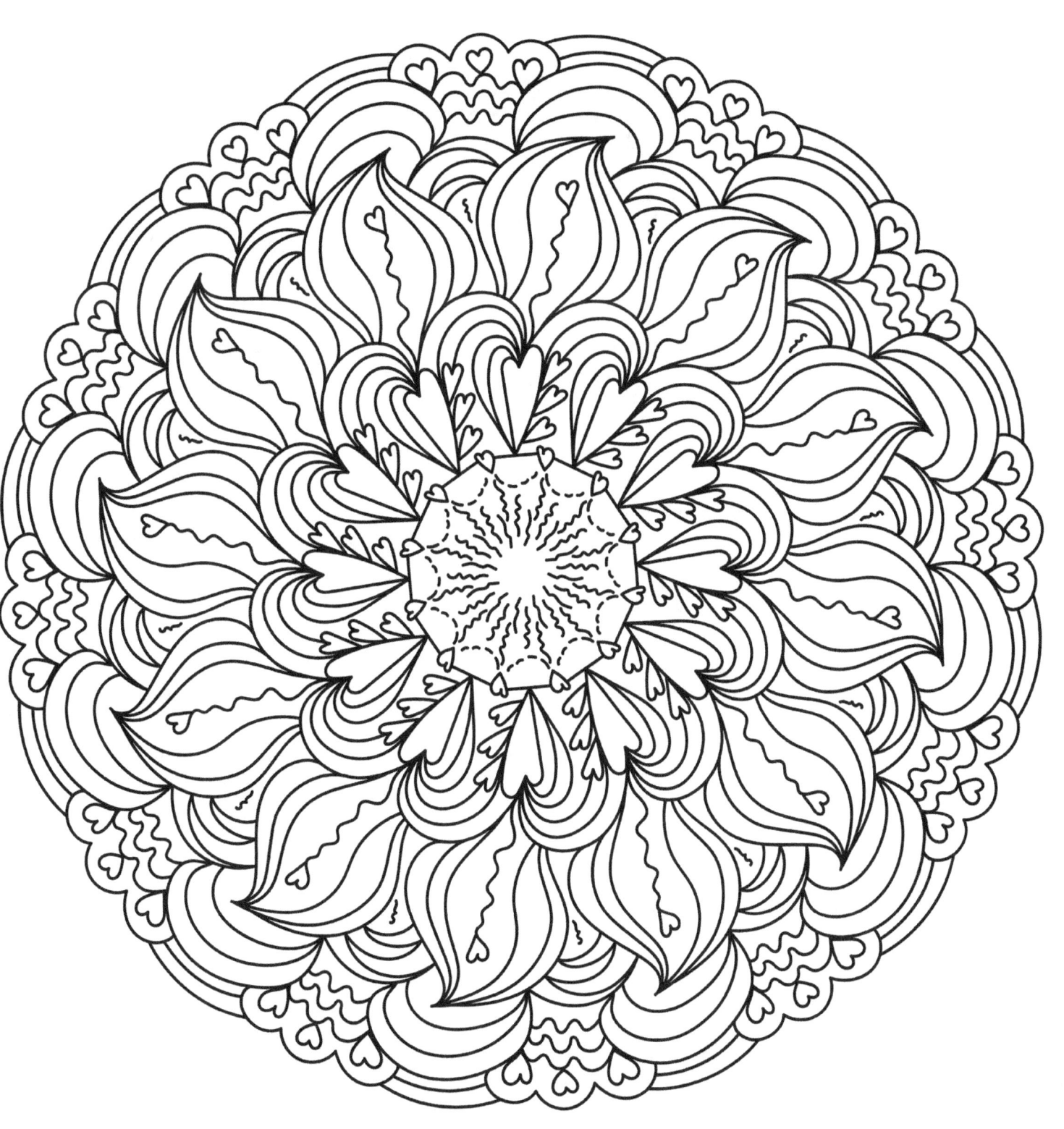

Mandala Hearts

by Little Mary

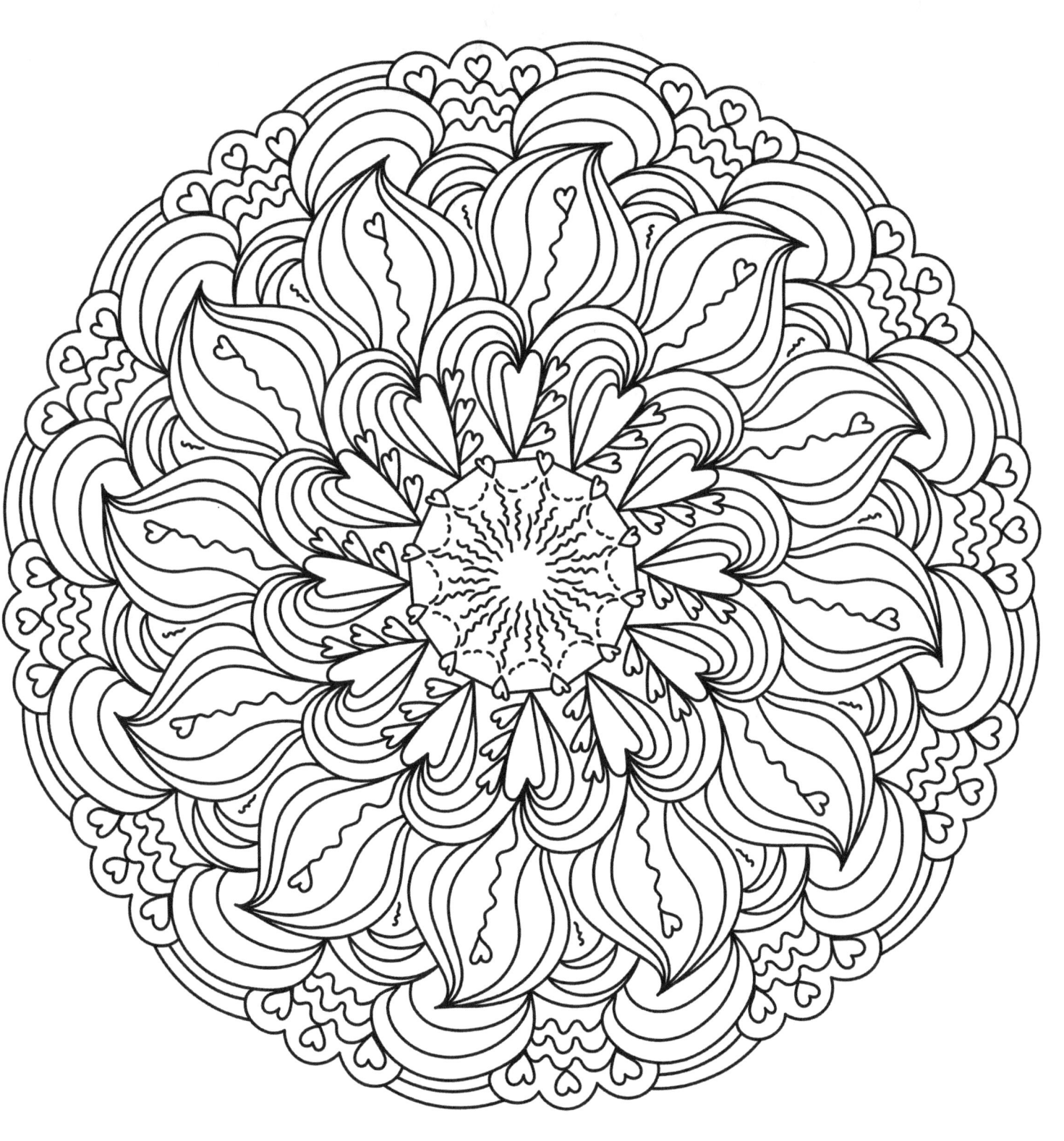

Mandala Hearts

by Little Mary

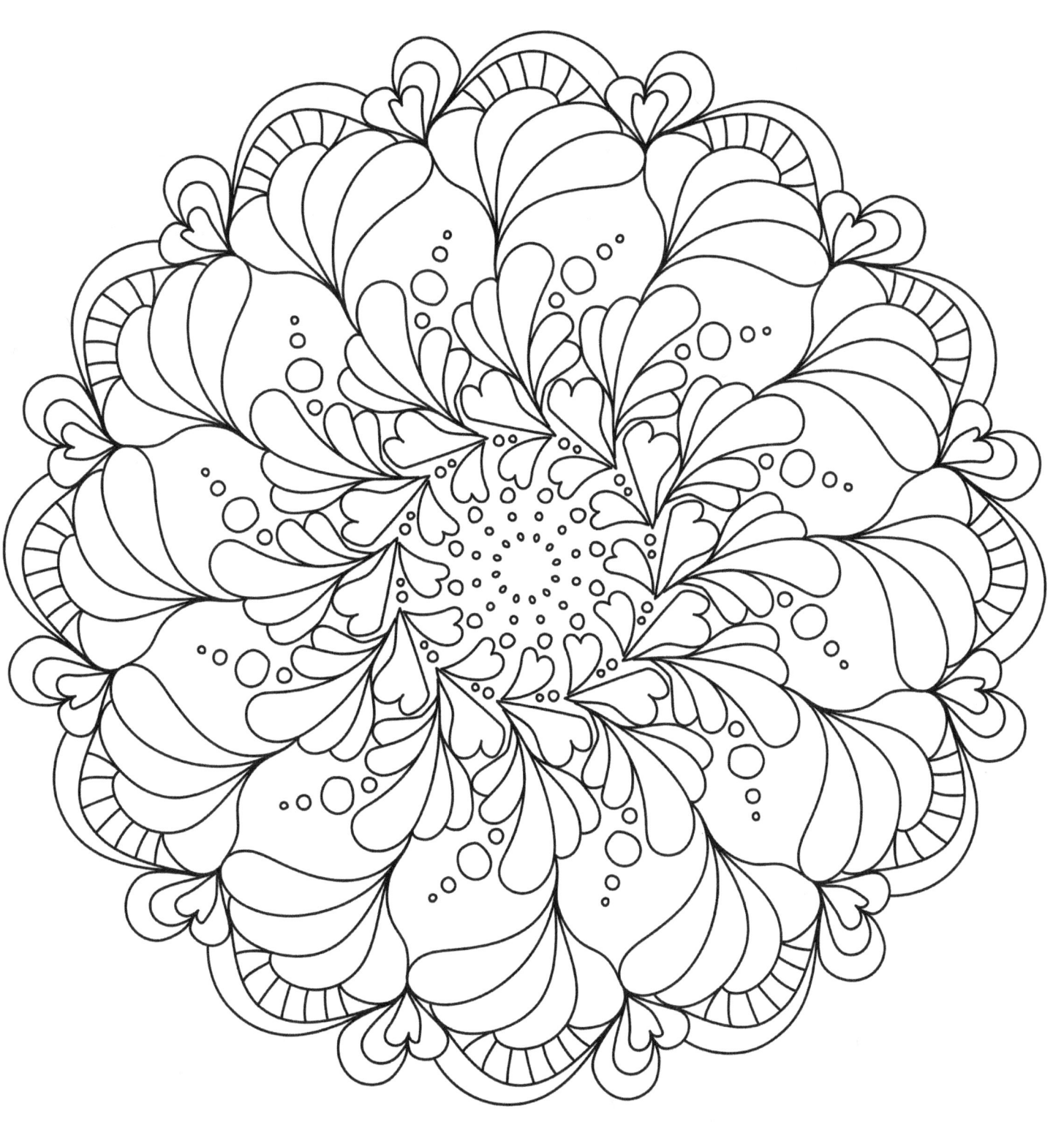

MANDALA HEARTS

by Little Mary